MW01711269

Beyond our Fears

Following Jesus in Times of Crisis

Faith & Life Resources
A division of Mennonite Publishing Network
Mennonite Church USA and
Mennonite Church Canada

Scottdale, Pennsylvania
Waterloo, Ontario

Beyond our Fears
Following Jesus in Times of Crisis (Guide for Leaders)

Faith & Life Resources gratefully acknowledges the financial support of Mennonite Disaster Service for this project. Thanks also to steering committee of Gordon Friesen and Lois Nickel of MDS, Janet Plenert of Mennonite Church Canada, and to the consulting group from across North America who offered ideas and support for the project.

International Standard Book Number: 978-0-8361-9479-1
Cover and book design by Merrill R. Miller
Cover Photo: iStockphoto/Helene Canada
Printed in USA

Orders and information:
USA: 800-245-7894
Canada: 800-631-6535
www.mpn.net

Contents

Introduction

For several years, medical authorities have been warning that the world is due to experience a serious flu virus on a global scale, equal to or greater than the flu pandemic of 1918. Despite our advanced medical technology, they warn, thousands of people will die, and many more will become sick. People will fear for their health. Naturally, people will want to protect themselves.

How will the church respond to a flu pandemic? How will it respond to any other kind of crisis—whether a pandemic, a natural disaster, or even an outbreak of violence or warfare? As Christians, do we have a plan? Will we retreat in fear, or are we ready to be God's light in the midst of suffering?

No one likes to think of disasters and pandemics. But crisis has always been a fact of human existence, and it can hit without warning. One problem for us in the North American church is that our technology and our wealth have led us to expect that we are immune; still, crises do come to our doorstep, as we have seen in Hurricane Katrina of 2005 and the SAARS crisis of 2003.

In other countries, people are living with crises that are hard for us to imagine. Our Christian brothers and sisters in sub-Sarahan Africa are coping with the AIDS pandemic, as well as other health problems such as malaria and malnutrition. Others deal with the unspeakable damage wrought in the tsunami of 2006 in Southeast Asia. Still others, living in Colombia, Iraq, and Palestine, live in the context of armed conflict.

This leader's guide, and the resources it accompanies, have been developed, not to raise fears among God's people, but to do the exact opposite: to prepare God's people to shine as God's light in the midst of such crises. It seeks to ensure that we will be people of healing and hope, not fear and self-preservation. Like the bridesmaids in Jesus' parable we will be well-supplied to light our lamps if and when hard times arrive.

How to use this guide

***Beyond our Fears* participant guide**

Don't Be Afraid

Orders and information:

USA: 800-245-7894
Canada: 800-631-6535
www.mpn.net

Beyond our Fears Guide for Leaders is meant to be used with two other core resources: *Beyond our Fears: Following Jesus in Times of Crisis*, a participant book of stories and Scripture reflections; and *Don't Be Afraid: Stories of Christians in Times of Trouble*, for middler children, ages 9-12. These two books are meant to be distributed widely among households in a congregation, not only as a study resource, but as inspiring literature to which individuals and families can turn again and again, especially during a time of crisis.

Settings. This book contains helps for at least four different kinds of congregational activities that may be organized separately, or in a coordinated emphasis on preparing for crisis:

- Adult studies (small group or Sunday school)
- Youth group (junior and senior high school Sunday school or mid-week)
- Children's activities (middler ages 9-12)
- Worship services

Most of the stories in *Don't Be Afraid* are fictionalized stories based on stories in *Beyond our Fears*, which opens possibilities for intergenerational discussion and study.

Mix, match, and adapt. Because of the interconnectedness of the activities, it is recommended that each group leader have a copy of this leader's guide. Especially in intergenerational activities, groups can borrow ideas and resources from various sections of the book. Here are just three examples:

- An adult group may find some of the youth activities useful, along with some of the worship resources.
- Worship leaders may use the first of the three worship

services to help the congregation anticipate pandemic or other crisis, but they may also wish to use other study material from this guide and the two books to fashion additional worship services around the themes of crisis preparedness.

- A youth group may draw on some of the children's activities (such as assembly of AIDS kits) or adult resources for additional ideas.

Hymn references. This book is designed for a variety of groups within the Mennonite family of churches and beyond. In the study guides and other resources, therefore, we occasionally suggest hymn and song titles but without reference to any particular hymnbook. We assume each group can find these, or alternatives, in the resources they use. For those who use *Hymnal: A Worship Book* and its supplements, however, there is a reference list.

Preface to the Youth and Adult Study Guides

These study guides—youth and adult versions—are designed to be used with the book, *Beyond our Fears: Following Jesus in Times of Crisis*. We encourage you, as the leader, to adapt the session plans to your group. The following suggestions will help you achieve the most benefit from the study.

Choose your setting. Ideally, this study will be done in **Sunday school, small group, youth group, or a retreat.** If your group has more than 20 members, split into two or more groups. Groups of more than ten tend to talk and interact less. Because of the interactive nature of the sessions, meet in a place where the group can sit in a circle.

Use the session material: The heart of these studies is the book *Beyond our Fears*, so each participant should have a copy. Participants will get more out of the sessions if they read the relevant chapter in preparation for each session. In some groups—especially among youth—that may be too much to expect of every participant. Still, the book will be an excellent personal resource both during and following the series.

Budget your time. These sessions work best in a time frame of an hour or more. Suggested times for each learning activity will help you budget time during the sessions. If you meet for less than an hour, consider taking more than four sessions to complete the series.

Read the material. Read through the whole session plan ahead of time, and determine which options you will follow. Each session begins with a helpful summary of the supplies and preparation tasks.

Prepare spiritually and emotionally. You are dealing with topics (disasters, disease, and other crises) that people don't normally want to talk about, especially when they're not experiencing them. Avoidance is natural. And yet, this study helps us confront fear with the compassion of Christ. It also reminds us that our brothers and sisters in the global Christian community are already dealing with some of these crises; this material helps us join them in spirit and support them in prayer.

Be creative. The session ideas here should work well in most groups. However, be creative when you feel certain ideas might not work in your group. If are leading an adult group, take a look at the leader guide for youth (page 39). Similarly, if you are leading a youth study, check the adult leader guide for more ideas.

Coordinate with other events in your church. These sessions can complement, or be adapted for, a congregation-wide emphasis on times of crisis and/or pandemic preparedness. If your congregation is not addressing these issues check with other leaders about the possibility of a sermon series, an intergenerational event, or a pandemic preparedness drive (see the resources on pages 102-3, particularly the website: www.churchpandemicresources.ca

Guide for
Adult Study Leader

1

Faith Overcomes Fear

Keep watch because you do not know the day or the hour.—Matthew 25:13

Faith is not just about trusting God to provide light when we find ourselves in the darkness of a crisis. Faith also means preparing, before the crisis comes, to carry God's light.

Story: Carmen almost loses her faith when Hurricane Katrina destroys her house in Pass Christian, Mississippi. When volunteers from Mennonite Disaster Service come to rebuild her house, she trusts God again and devotes her time to helping others in need.

Bible text: Matthew 25:1-13—The parable of the bridesmaids

Supplies

- *Beyond our Fears* book for each person
- Hymnals or songbooks
- Bibles
- Colored candies (of at least six colors) enough for each person to have two or three (for opening)
- Flip chart or whiteboard and markers
- Large white pillar candle, matches (for the closing option)

Advance preparation

1. Read through the introduction and the contents of *Beyond our Fears* so that you are familiar with the flow of topics over the next sessions.

2. Read and reflect on the story, the Scripture, and the Scripture meditation for Chapter 1 in *Beyond our Fears*.
3. Set up the meeting space. If possible arrange chairs in a circle or semi-circle.
4. Collect recommended articles and other resources about pandemics and weather-related disasters.

Opening (10 minutes)

1. Welcome people as they gather. Tell them what you hope will happen during this series. Encourage their participation through the four sessions as each builds on the previous one. Explain how this session will work. Take time for introductions if needed.
2. Pass around a dish of candies inviting each person to take two or three. Then present the scenarios below, inviting each person with the corresponding color to answer. Don't comment on the answers, just jot them down on the flip chart or white board.
    - If you have a red candy, name or describe what you would call a *natural disaster*.
    - If you have a yellow candy, tell how you would define *disaster*.
    - If you have a green candy, name or describe what you would call a *pandemic*.
    - If you have a purple candy, tell how you would define *pandemic*.
    - If you have a brown candy, name the main *emotion* you would feel if you knew a natural disaster was about to happen.
    - If you have an orange candy, name the main *emotion* you would feel if you knew a pandemic was likely to happen.

Distribute copies of *Beyond our Fears*. Say something like: *During these sessions we will explore the church's response to troubling events that happen around the world as well as close to home. Today we begin with a story about a natural disaster, Hurricane Katrina. We'll also explore a Bible text that may give us insights on how we as Christians and as a congregation can prepare ourselves to be faithful in times of fear and uncertainty.*

4. If you are a singing group, sing "When peace, like a river." This hymn was written by Horatio G. Spafford in 1876. He lost his real estate fortune in the Chicago fire of 1871. In 1873 four daughters died in a shipwreck, and in 1880 his son died of scarlet fever. Through the pain and sorrow, he penned the words, "It is well with my soul."

Reflect on the story (10 minutes)

1. Read or summarize the story, "I Thought God Would Take Care of Us" (page 7 *Beyond our Fears*).
2. Invite responses to the story:
   - How similar or different would your reactions have been to those of Carmen? How did the church respond to the devastation of the hurricane? (At this point you may wish to say a few words about the ministry of Mennonite Disaster Service; see the sidebar on page 11, *Beyond our Fears*.)
   - What can Carmen's story teach us about trusting God?
   - How does one prepare for such devastation?

Reflect on the Scripture text (10–15 minutes)

1. Open Bibles to Matthew 25:1-13 and read the parable of the bridesmaids. For dramatic effect, assign parts to different readers: narrator, shouter, foolish bridesmaid, wise bridesmaid, and bridegroom.
2. Invite initial responses to the parable:
   - Which of the bridesmaids do you identify with the most—the ones with barely enough oil or the ones with plenty?
   - What surprises or disturbs you about the parable?
   - What do you think is the point of this parable?

3. Create a "Top Ten Reasons" chart. Divide a piece of chart paper into two columns headed "Not Prepared" and "Prepared." List the reasons that the bridesmaids might give for having just enough oil and the reasons for having more than enough oil.

   Mention the point that Pam Driedger makes about each group of bridesmaids exhibiting a kind of "faith"—one waits until there is a crisis and asks God to intervene, and the other prepares ahead of time.

   Option: If the group is large, work on the chart in small groups.

Integrate (15–20 minutes)

1. Ask the group to imagine that they are preparing for potential disasters. Based on your Top Ten Reasons chart, ask them:

   - What reasons do we give for preparing or not preparing for a disaster of major proportions? Add these reasons to the chart.
   - How do we prepare differently when our motivation is based on faith rather than fear?
   - What fears must we first face or overcome in order to prepare ourselves for the worst?
   - How can we prepare our children for such crises in a way the inspires faith and hope in them?

2. Prepare to be faithful. Read this statement to the group:

   Government health organizations in both the United States and Canada have indicated their desire for churches to be involved in the work of preparing for a pandemic. But most churches do not talk about potential future disasters, preferring to leave the future, at least the unpleasant elements of the future, to God. Jesus' parable of the ten bridesmaids challenges us to be prepared for the unexpected.

3. Ask the group to think about what they need so they are prepared to serve Christ faithfully in the event of a major crisis. Ask them to think about the following questions. They should not answer out loud.

- What do you need from God?
- What do you need from the congregation?
- What does it mean for you to be faithful and ready?

Option: If a participant has experienced a disaster or some other devastating crisis, now would be a good time for them to share from a faith perspective. What helped them remain faithful to God? How was God faithful to them? What helped them to face their fears in the situation? What did they learn that will help them to face future crises?

4. On the flip chart or white board, jot down ways in which people in your church can help each other to be faithful to God in times of disasters. What resources will help us stay strong in the midst of chaos and stress?

   Option: Post this list and add suggestions as you work through the next sessions.

5. Tell the group that during the next three sessions you will focus on health crises: HIV/AIDS, SARS, and a potential influenza pandemic. You will reflect together on the stories and Scripture texts given in *Beyond our Fears* to become aware of issues people face when dealing with crises. You will talk about the importance of facing this subject, even though it may feel uncomfortable. As a group you will learn to be prepared—along with your families and your congregation—to respond out of faith, not fear. We may know how to respond to natural disasters (MDS is a wonderful example); can we also learn how to respond well in times of health crises?

6. Pray. When we believe that God is present in all of life's circumstances we trust that God will be with us in times of crises. In light of this conviction, either sing or read the words to the song, "When the storms of life are raging" by Charles A. Tindley, verses 1-2—or another hymn that may be appropriate.

   Option: invite silent and audible prayers from the group, seeking courage to be prepared to serve Christ in any kind of disaster.

End with a prayer for this group, asking God to stand by us as we learn how to respond to crises out of faith, not fear.

Closing (5 minutes)

Remind the group to take their books home and use them between sessions. Encourage them to read Chapter 1 as a review and Chapter 2 in preparation for the next session. Suggest that they make notes on the readings and bring their questions to the group. Encourage them to pray that God would enable the church to be faithful witnesses to God's love, not only in times of crisis, but in times of watchfulness and preparation.

Option for a closing ritual to be repeated at the end of each session.

Sit quietly for a moment, collecting your thoughts from the session.

Light the white pillar candle.

Say: *The light of Christ never goes out. This candle can remind us that God will be with us as we prepare to face a crisis that we'd rather not think about. Know that our Christian faith can sustain us and our community of faith can be a means of support. We are on this learning journey together, and the light of Christ precedes us.*

Choose one of the following options:

- Pass the candle carefully to members in the group as you sing verse three of the song, "Will you let me be your servant" or another song about service.
- Invite each person to say, as they pass the candle, "_____*(name)*____ let the light of Christ guide you in the night-time of your fear."

(*Note:* If the group is larger, have one person hold the candle.)

As you blow out the candle at the end, tell the group that, although the flame is extinguished, the Spirit of God goes with us now as we go and serve in our world.

2

Compassion Overcomes Blame

Neither this man nor his parents sinned; he was born blind so that God's works might be revealed in him.—John 9:3

It is natural for us to ask who or what is responsible for a crisis. The Scriptures, however, call us to focus on the opportunities we have to show God's grace and compassion, regardless of who is at fault.

Story: Nothando and her friend Abeni find their lives turned upside down by the AIDS epidemic in Zimbabwe, southern Africa. Despite the prejudices and fears of their family and friends, they choose to care for those who are suffering, regardless of their background.

Bible text: John 9:1-34—The man born blind

Supplies

- Extra participant books for any newcomers
- Bibles
- Hymnals
- Pillar candle (for optional closing)
- Modeling clay or play dough, small piece for each person
- Blank paper and thin markers or pencil crayons

Advance preparation

1. Read through the entire session, including the participant's book.

2. Take time to read and reflect on the Bible story for this session.
3. If you plan to read the Scripture story as a drama, assign parts ahead of time.
4. Find the prayer of Francis of Assisi, also known as the song, "Make me a channel of your peace," in a hymnal, on the Internet, or as a recording.
5. For the Integrate section, visit the pandemic preparedness website of Mennonite Church Canada (www.churchpandemicresources.ca) and browse pages that might be helpful for this section. If your meeting place is wired to the Internet, consider hooking up a projector to introduce the site to your group. If not, point it out on page 38 of their books.
6. If you choose the Internet option in the Integrate section, set up the computer and projector, and have the pandemic website ready to access.

Opening (10 minutes)

1. Welcome people as they gather. Make introductions as needed. For newcomers, review the subject matter of the series.
2. Sculpture: Grace and Compassion.
    - Have the participants form groups of three.
    - Each group picks one person to be the "sculptor." The other two will be the clay. Each group must create a sculpture that depicts *compassion*.
    - The sculptor then shapes the other two participants into a statue by moving their limbs into place.
    - Allow a few minutes for sculpting, then have each group present the sculpture to the larger group.
    - Invite some reflection on the different ways that compassion is interpreted.
3. Mention that this session's focus is on moving beyond the blame game to sharing the love and compassion of Jesus. Through song and prayer we open ourselves to hear the gentle nudging of God to be compassionate to those who

are suffering. Sing or read the prayer of Francis of Assisi, "Make me a channel of God's peace."

Reflect on the story (10–12 minutes)

Read or summarize the story, "Choosing to Love" (page 15 of *Beyond our Fears*). Invite the group to comment on their reaction to the story.

- How were Nothando and Abeni channels of God's peace?
- How did you feel about the decisions they made to care for people with AIDS?
- Are some people more deserving of care than others?

Reflect on the Scripture text (10 minutes)

1. Read John 9:1-34.

   Option: Have different people read the parts of narrator, Jesus, blind man, and parents. Divide the rest of the group into parts of the crowd, disciples, neighbors, Pharisees, and Jews.

   Option: If the group has read the text ahead of time, summarize the story.

2. Invite responses to the story:

   - Why was it important to the Pharisees and the disciples that someone be blamed for the man's blindness?
   - With which of the characters in this story do you identify? Explain why.
   - What message did Jesus give to his followers about suffering?

Integrate (15–20 minutes)

1. Ponder and Discuss. Say something like: *Jesus' disciples looked for a reason that would explain why God would make someone blind. The human desire to find a reason for suffering is not new. If we can find a reason we can explain the suffering and make it seem just. Jesus invites his followers to look at suffering in a new way—one which focuses on the opportunities to show compassion to those who suffer, no matter what the reason.*

- What connections do you see between the Zimbabwe story and the Scripture story?
- How were grace and compassion evident in these stories?

2. Prepare to be faithful.

Say something like: *The HIV/AIDS epidemic in Zimbabwe and other parts of Africa may seem too distant to affect the way we live our daily lives—even though we might feel compassion in our hearts. We may have donated money or AIDS kits to a charitable organization devoted to AIDS programs. But how would we be prepared for a large scale crisis close to home?*

Read or summarize the following quote from a document of the Canadian government, on preparing for an influenza pandemic. It says:

> A pandemic is a worldwide outbreak of a specific disease which affects a large proportion of the population. There is no influenza pandemic activity anywhere in the world at this time, but scientists agree there will be a global outbreak of influenza (flu) sooner or later . . .
>
> It is very difficult to predict the impact of a pandemic, since no one knows how the virus would behave or how serious the pandemic would be. During a severe flu season, as many as 8,000 Canadians die from influenza and its complications; on average there are 4,000 deaths from annual flu. In a moderately severe pandemic, it is estimated that between 11,000 and 58,000 deaths may occur in Canada. These numbers are based on an assumption that the virus would cause illness in 15 to 35 per cent of the population.
>
> In addition to deaths, a pandemic may cause significant illness and social disruption. It is important for Canadian families to plan ahead for a pandemic, because services provided by hospitals and clinics may be reduced or unavailable. Also, grocery stores and pharmacies may have limited supplies and banks may close.*

---

*www.hc-sc.gc.ca/hl-vs/iyh-vsv/diseases-maladies/pandem-eng.php (The U.S. government website www.pandemicflu.gov/index.html contains similar information.) See the FAQ section under pandemic influenza.

Option: If your setting is wired to the Internet, go to http://www.churchpandemicresources.ca to begin an exploration of what it means to be a caring faith community. Pay particular attention to the page that discusses caring before a pandemic. Identify some steps that you might take individually and/or as a congregation to prepare to extend healing and hope to people who are particularly vulnerable.

3. Hands-on reflection.
   - Hand out pieces of modeling clay or paper and markers.
   - Ask participants to sculpt or draw something that symbolizes compassion, in light of their reflection on these stories.
   - After a few minutes of silent work, invite them to share about their symbol or what they were thinking about as they worked with their hands.

4. Prayer.
   - Say: *We can trust that God will guide us as we make difficult decisions about care-giving and coping in a time of crisis. Our faith can sustain us as it did the women in Zimbabwe.*
   - Invite the group to stand and respond to this blessing by Teresa of Avila. As they hear the words *hands*, *feet*, and *eyes*, ask them to move them in some way.

     Christ has no body now on earth but yours;

     Yours are the only hands with which Christ can do his work,

     Yours are the only feet with which Christ can go about the world,

     Yours are the only eyes through which Christ's compassion can shine forth upon a troubled world.

     Christ has no body on earth now but yours.

Closing (5 minutes)

Remind the group to use *Beyond our Fears* between sessions. They should read Chapter 3 for next time, along with the story of Bishop Cyprian (page 33). Suggest that they make notes on the readings and bring their questions to the session. Encourage them to pray that God would enable the church to be faithful witnesses to God's love, not only in times of crisis that may or may not occur, but in times of watchfulness and preparation.

Option for closing ritual: see the instructions on page 18.

3

Service Overcomes Self-Preservation

Let each of you look not to your own interests, but to the interests of others. Let the same mind be in you that was in Christ Jesus . . .—Philippians 2:4-7

Our human reaction is to escape or to build walls of protection around ourselves when our health or safety is threatened. God calls us to be prudent, but also to follow Jesus, who gave his own life in service to others.

Story: A strange disease, SARS, threatens to spread throughout Toronto in the spring of 2003. Amanda, a nurse, must wear protective clothing at work, and is quarantined at home. But she knows that she is doing what God has called her to do: care for sick people, no matter what the personal risks.

Bible text: Philippians 2:1-11—God comes as a human servant

Supplies

- Participant books
- Hymnals or songbooks
- Option: Recording of the song, "Here I am, Lord" (text and Music by Daniel Schutte and New Dawn Music, 1981)
- Bibles
- Rope, or masking or duct tape
- Flip chart or white board and markers
- Pillar candle, if you choose the closing option

Advance preparation

1. Read through the entire session, including Chapter 3 of *Beyond our Fears*.
2. Read and reflect on the Bible text for this session.
3. With rope or tape, mark a line on the floor long enough for the whole group to stand on side by side. If you have a large group, make several lines. Place a piece of paper at one end of the line with "very much so" written on it. Put another piece of paper at the other end of the line with "not at all" written on it.
4. Ask a group member to come prepared to read the Scripture text in a conventional translation and in a contemporary paraphrase (such as *The Message*).
5. On the flip chart or white board, draw a Venn diagram: two large circles that overlap in the center. Print these headings: "Practical Human Wisdom" (left) and "The Mind of Christ" (right), "The Best of Both" (center).

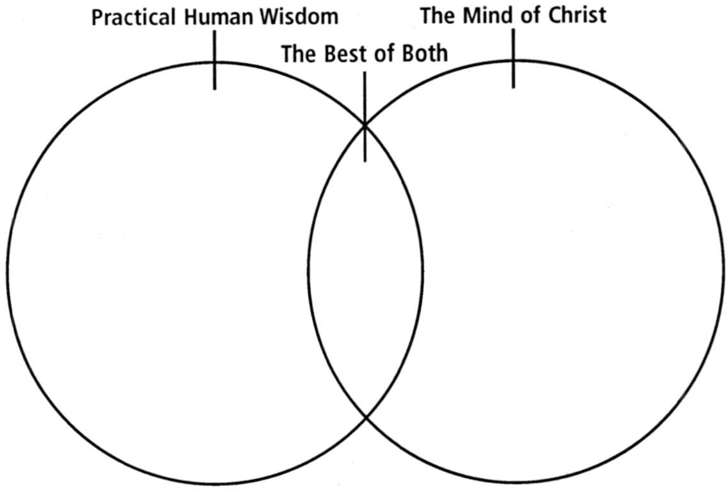

6. Slips of paper, on which are written roles in the early church (see Integrate).

Opening (10 minutes)

1. Welcome people as they gather. Make introductions as needed. For newcomers, review the subject matter of the series.

2 Explain that the line on the floor represents their answers to a series of questions. Put you "very much so" sign at the left end of the line, and the "not at all" sign at the right end. You will make a statement, and the participants will place themselves at the place on the line that represents their level of agreement. There is no right or wrong answer. Start with a few fun statements such as, "I am a nice person" or "I am a safe driver" so they become comfortable with the process.

   - I am a risk taker.
   - I give homeless people cash.
   - I would donate a kidney to a close relative.
   - I am a religious fanatic.
   - I would put my life on the line for a stranger.

   Without commenting on the choices people made, reflect on the experience itself: Was if difficult to respond to the questions? If so, what made it difficult? Were people surprised by the choices that were made?

3. Say that this session is about choosing to serve God without fear. It looks at our motivation to remain faithful followers of Jesus in the midst of a pandemic or disaster.

   Option: Sing or listen to the song, "Here I am, Lord" by Daniel Schutte, or another song about service to God.

Reflect on the story (10 minutes)

1. Read or summarize the story, "Choosing to Serve."
2. Invite responses to the story using some or all of these questions:
   - What feelings does this story stir up in you? Explain.
   - What motivated Amanda and Joanna to take the risks they did?

- What roles did the faith community and family members play in their decisions?
- If you are a healthcare provider, what issues does this story raise for you personally?
- If you are a relative or close friend of a healthcare provider, how would you respond?

Reflect on the Scripture text (10 minutes)

1. Ask your reader to read Philippians 2:1-11 in the traditional version. Encourage the group to listen for phrases or words that stand out for them. Then read the same text from the contemporary version. Pause in silence for a moment or two.
2. Invite responses to the text as heard in both readings.
    - What words or phrases stood out for you in the first reading?
    - Did the second reading change your understanding?
    - What does it mean to have the mind of Christ?
    - The early church used some of these verses as a hymn. Jesus' sacrificial living guided their way of living in the world. What value does this passage have for Christians today?

Say something like: *In today's society we are often encouraged to take care of ourselves first. Large organizations devote a significant amount of time to the issue of risk reduction. Anyone who is willing to give one's life for their faith is a fanatic. So how do we understand the call of Philippians 2, which encourages us to be like Christ—willing to risk our lives for the sake of others?*

Integrate (15–20 minutes)

1. Ponder and discuss. To explore our motivation for serving in risky situations, ask the group to fill in the Venn diagram.
    - On the left, under the title "Practical Human Wisdom" write reasons that secular thinking would give for choosing not to risk one's life in service during a pandemic.

- On the right, under "The Mind of Christ" write reasons that Christians who have the mind of Christ would give for choosing to risk one's life.
- In the overlapping space, under "The Best of Both," write motivations that reflect both secular and Christian perspectives.

Option: If the group has more than eight people, break into small groups: three groups can each take one section of the diagram, or groups can work at all three sections.

2. Ask:

- What differences would you expect to find between a secular response and a Christian response to taking such a risk?
- Who should be expected to care for the sick during a pandemic or highly contagious epidemic?
- What fears must we face if we are willing to serve God faithfully in such a crisis?

3. Prepare to be faithful.

- Review the choices made by early Christians during the epidemic in the year 251 as noted in the Scripture meditation (*Beyond our Fears*, page 24) and the story of Bishop Cyprian (page 33). As a result of the Christians' willingness to risk their lives at this time, people took notice and the church grew.
- Introduce the following activity by saying something like: *Let's imagine that we are part of a Christian community living in Rome or Carthage during this time. The devastating epidemic is getting worse, people are fleeing the city. The medical experts among the pagans are insisting that the only possible response to this illness is to get as far away from it as possible. The question before us is what we should do as a church. We know that the Christians chose to risk their lives in service in the face of fear.*

  Ask the participants to assume the roles listed below (feel free to copy and cut into strips) and imagine the conversation and thinking that might have encouraged and challenged the Christians to stay and to serve the sick. Assign the roles, then allow the group some quiet time to get into their roles. Ask them to tell the group how their character would act if he or she were guided by the mind of Christ Jesus.

- A young widow with three small children who has recently become a Christian.
- A merchant who has given half his possessions to the church community.
- A former soldier who gave up his profession when he joined the Christian church.
- A teacher who believes that all of Christian faith is summed up in the hymn found in Philippians 2:6-11.
- A widower who is nearing the end of his life.
- A man who trained as a doctor and knows that there is no cure for this illness.
- The church treasurer.
- The pastor.

After the discussion, invite people to respond to their feelings and the way the discussion evolved. How would it be similar or different if they played themselves and they were living on the edge of a contemporary flu pandemic?

- *Option:* Use the following scenario instead of, or in addition to, the scenario above.

  A pandemic flu is spreading rapidly through North America. There have been no cases in your community but a hospital in a nearby city has had an unusually high number of cases. Many of the staff have also been infected. The hospital has sent out a request to health professionals in neighboring areas asking them to come and help. Two nurses and two doctors in your congregation have come to your Sunday school class asking for help to discern whether or not they should volunteer. One is a single parent of teenagers. One is married with young children. One is married with grown children and one is single.

Note: this scenario is also an option in Session 4. If you use it here, you will not use it in Session 4—unless you want to go into it in greater depth.

4. Prayer. Being a Christian during a time of crisis is risky business. It is only with God's help and the support of the Christian community that we can stay strong and faithful. Sing a song that encourages faith in the time of risk, such as:
   - "I am weak and I need thy strength" by Doris M. Akers 1953
   - "Help us to help each other" by Charles Wesley
   - "Will you come and follow me?" John Bell and Graham Maule 1987

Closing (5 minutes)

- Remind the group to use *Beyond our Fears* between sessions. They should read Chapter 4 for next time. Suggest that they make notes on the readings and bring their questions to the session. Encourage them to pray that God would enable the church to be faithful witnesses to God's love, not only in times of crisis that may or may not happen, but in times of watchfulness and preparation.
- *Option for closing ritual*: see the instructions on page 18.

4

Living in Hope Overcomes Darkness

If you . . . satisfy the needs of the afflicted, then your light shall rise in the darkness and your gloom be like the noonday.—Isaiah 58:10

The light of God will shine in the darkness of any crisis as the church participates faithfully and courageously in God's restoring work.

Story: In 1666, two local church leaders convince the people of Eyam, England, to voluntarily quarantine their village to keep the bubonic plague from spreading to neighboring communities. Today, the village is still remembered as a beacon of sacrificial love.

Bible text: Isaiah 58:6-12—God's promise of restoration

Supplies

- Participant books
- Hymnals
- Bibles
- Pillar candle
- Small tea lights or floating candles (opening)
- Small candles with cardboard holders
- Glass bowl large enough to hold the pillar candle and a tea light for each person
- Water
- Book of matches or a lighter
- Flip chart, markers

Advance preparation

1. Read through the entire session, including Chapter 4 of the participant's book.
2. Fill the bowl with water and place the pillar candle in the middle of it. Set the bowl in a visible and accessible place. Place matches and tea lights around the bowl.
3. Ask someone to prepare a dramatic reading of the Scripture text.
4. Divide the chart paper into two columns. On one column write "Our Actions," on the other, "God's Promises."
5. Explore the on-line pandemic preparedness website developed by Mennonite Church Canada: www.churchpandemicresources.ca Be sure to check out the congregational preparedness documents. If you think your group is ready for it, choose option A in the Integrate section below. Download and copy the document "Getting a Congregational Dialogue Started" (a version of which is included in this guide on pages 98-100). Choose several practical questions to discuss in your group and think through the follow-up. Your time will be too short to respond to the questions in depth; be prepared to appoint a small group to take further action following the series.

Opening (10 minutes)

1. Welcome people as they gather. Make introductions as needed. For newcomers, review the subject matter of the series. Note that this is the last session of the series. Darken the room if you can.
2. Say something like: *The topics we are discussing can cast a shadow over us as we think of potentially dire situations in which we could find ourselves, our families, and our entire community. At the same time, as Christians, we know that God cares and is present in our dark times. Light the Christ candle as a symbol of that presence—a reminder that to live in hope and faith means to take risks and to face the future knowing that God will sustain us.*

   As a way to express a desire to be faithful to God, invite

adult guide

group members to light a tea light candle and place it in the bowl of water. Encourage them to name a hope they have as they light the candle. Note what happens: as more candles are lit, the darkness is dispelled. Brighten up the room again by turning on more lights.

3. Sing a song of hope, such as "In the bulb there is a flower" by Natalie Sleeth.

Reflect on the story (10 minutes)

1. Read or summarize the story, "A Village Quarantines Itself" (page 28 of *Beyond our Fears*).
2. Invite responses from prior reading and these questions:
   - How do you respond emotionally to the story from England?
   - Why do you think the villagers responded as they did?
   - Does this sacrifice inspire you? Why or why not?
   - Do you think that the actions of the villagers could be replicated in your geographical community? Why or why not?

Reflect on the Scripture text (10 minutes)

1. Ask the reader to read Isaiah 58:6-12 while the group listens carefully.
2. Ask the group to open their Bibles to the text.
3. Ask the following questions:
   - What struck you as you heard the text?
   - What comments do you have about the Scripture reflection in your book? [This assumes participants have read Chapter 4. If they haven't, make reference to one or two points.]
   - According to the prophet Isaiah, what actions of the people bring light into the darkness? [List these actions on the flip chart]
   - What does God promise if the people act in obedience and trust? [List these as well.]

adult guide

4. Divide into smaller groups or pairs and ask the participants to consider the Scripture text in light of a pandemic scenario.

   - Ask them to think of several specific actions that they could take that would bring God's light into the darkness of a pandemic.
   - For each action, consider a promise of God that would bring hope to the caregivers. These can be added to the lists on the flip chart.
   - *Option:* Create a unison reading out of this assignment. Have the pairs write their actions and promises as "If-then" sentences, similar to the biblical verses. Example: If you feed a child weakend by the flu, then God's light will shine in the darkness." Each pair will contribute to the litany.

Integrate (15–20 minutes)

1. Ponder and discuss

   Say something like: *The stories and Scripture in this series suggest that the church and God's people can bring light in the darkness through acts of compassion and courage in the face of disaster. When we move beyond our fears and trust that God will light our way, we can offer hope to a world that is falling apart. The four stories tell of real people who chose to bring light in the midst of despair because of their Christian convictions.* Discuss:

   - How have these stories inspired you?
   - What did you learn from this study that has strengthened your faith?
   - What fears are still lurking?
   - Does awareness about potential crises (pandemics or disasters) increase or decrease your fear? Does it strengthen or weaken your faith?
   - Do you think our congregation could make the same choice that the villagers did to stay at home to contain the disease, even though it meant sacrificing their lives?

2. Prepare to be faithful.

   Choose one of the two options below. *Option:* Whether you choose the first or second option consider asking for volunteers to form a task force to do further work on recommendations for your congregation's leaders.

   A. *Congregational pandemic preparedness checklist.* If the group is ready, read over the pandemic preparedness document "Getting a Congregational Dialogue Started" (see Advance Preparation above) and go through the points one by one, asking what practical steps your congregation might take to be prepared for a pandemic. You may wish to divide the group and each discuss a section of the document.

   B. *Imagine what you would do.* Consider the following scenarios in light of what the group has experienced in these sessions. Assign them to groups to discuss and report back to the whole group what responses you might give.

      Scenario #1: Your neighbor calls to say that her husband has been diagnosed with a new strain of flu virus which is highly contagious and for which there is no reliable treatment. She is now running a fever and feeling very weak. So far her children ages 4, 6 and 10 have shown no symptoms. She has called to ask if you will take care of her children.

      Scenario #2: Joe, a member of your congregation, is a spiritual care provider (chaplain) at a local hospital. The hospital has had numerous cases of the flu pandemic that is devastating the country. So far the flu has been contained to four hospital wards. Because spiritual care is not considered an essential service, Joe is given a choice to work on these wards or avoid them. If he chooses to work there, he will need to go into home quarantine. Joe asks your Sunday school class to help him make a faithful decision.

      Scenario #3: A pandemic flu is raging through the country. Many homeless shelters have shut down and soup kitchens have closed because there are not enough volunteers. More than a dozen people have called your church in the past week looking for food and a place to stay. Several are coughing or wheezing. A congregational meeting has been called to discuss what your church would be willing to do. You are on the church council.

Scenario #4: Make up a scenario that is specific to your congregation and the members of the group. Is there a group of people you know who would be particularly vulnerable during a time of crisis? How can you minister to them?

Discuss: What steps toward pandemic preparedness would you recommend to your congregation's leaders? Note them and be sure to pass them on.

Closing (5 minutes)

1. Thank the group for their courage to participate in this study. Encourage them to continue to pray for direction as they decide how they can prepare themselves and their families for crisis—spiritually, physically, and emotionally. As a closing, indicate that you will bless each other in being the light of Christ—in any crises they face, whether large or small.
2. The following is an adaptation of the repeated closing option (as outlined in Session 1, page 18).
    - If possible, dim the lights so only the candles are lighting your space.
    - Gather in a circle and distribute small candles to each person.
    - Take the pillar candle from the basin of water, light it, and as you hold it, say: Our prayer is that we will be faithful in times of crisis, hopeful in the midst of despair, and light in the shadows of hard time.
    - Invite each person to come and light his or her candle from the larger candle. As they light their little candles, offer each this blessing: "[*Name*,] your faith will be God's light in the darkness."
    - As a prayer, sing, "This little light of mine"
    - Allow each person to bless their neighbor with a word

of encouragement, such as: "[*Name*,] let the light of Christ give you hope. Go and serve our God."

- As they blow out the candles, remind them that although the candle flame is extinguished, the Spirit of God goes with us to help us serve and love God's people.

Guide for
Youth Study Leader

1

Faith Overcomes Fear

Keep watch because you do not know the day or the hour.—Matthew 25:13

Faith is not just about trusting God to provide light when we find ourselves in the darkness of a crisis. Faith also means preparing, before the crisis comes, to carry God's light.

Story: Carmen almost loses her faith when Hurricane Katrina destroys her house in Pass Christian, Mississippi. When volunteers from Mennonite Disaster Service come to rebuild her house, she trusts God again and devotes her time to helping others in need.

Bible text: Matthew 25:1-13—The parable of the bridesmaids

youth guide

Supplies

- Hymnals
- Bibles
- *Beyond our Fears* books, one for each person
- The following words on large pieces of paper, one word (or phrase) per piece: *Horrible, Awful, No Good, Very Bad, Day*
- Flip chart or whiteboard and markers
- A roll of thin rope and a scissors
- *Optional:* white candle for optional closing
- Photos of destruction from Hurricane Katrina. One way to provide these, if you have internet access for your class, is to go online and search for Hurricane Katrina photos and view them online as a class.

Advance preparation

1. Read through the introduction and the contents of *Beyond our Fears* so that you are familiar with the flow of topics over the next sessions.
2. Read and reflect on the story, the Scripture, and the Scripture meditation for Session 1 in *Beyond our Fears* (page 7).
3. Set up the meeting space. If possible arrange chairs in a circle or semi-circle.
4. Invite a woman to your class who can tell or read the story "I thought God would take care of us" in a dramatic way.

Opening (10 minutes)

1. Welcome members as they arrive.
2. Give five people the pieces of paper with the words, and ask them to arrange themselves in the "correct order," reflecting the title of the book *Alexander and the Terrible, Horrible, No Good, Very Bad Day* by Judith Viorst. Invite volunteers to share about a "horrible awful no good very bad day" that they have experienced.
    - Ask the person holding the "horrible" sign to define or name a natural disaster, and write that on the flip chart or white board.
    - Ask the person with the "awful" sign to define a disaster and write that down.
    - Ask the person with the "no good" sign to define a pandemic and write that down.
    - Ask the person with the "very bad" sign to say how they would feel if they knew a natural disaster was about to happen to them and write it down.
    - Ask the person with the "day" sign to say how they would feel if they knew a pandemic was likely to happen and write it down.
3. Say: *For the next four sessions/weeks, we're going to talk about crises that have happened or could happen in our world. We're going to look at how Christians have*

responded, or might be called to respond in the future. Today we begin with a story from a natural disaster, Hurricane Katrina.

Reflect on the story (15 minutes)

1. Read or tell the story "I thought God would take care of us" (page 7, *Beyond our Fears*).
2. Look at Hurricane Katrina photos. Ask students to imagine how it would feel if these were photos of their home or their community.
3. Break into pairs and discuss:
    - How similar or different would your reactions have been to those of Carmen in the story?
    - How did the church respond to the devastation of the hurricane? [At this point you may wish to say a few words about the ministry of Mennonite Disaster Service; see the sidebar on page 11, *Beyond our Fears*.]
    - What can Carmen's story teach us about trusting in God?
    - How can we prepare for an unexpected crisis—whether a natural disaster, a health pandemic, or a violent incident?

Reflect on the Scripture text (10–15 minutes)

1. Assign these roles to different readers: narrator, shouter, foolish bridesmaid, wise bridesmaid, and bridegroom.
2. Open Bibles to Matthew 25:1-13 and act out the story.
3. Break into pairs with someone you haven't talked to today and share your answers to the following questions:
    - Which of the bridesmaids do you identify with the most—the ones with barely enough oil or the ones with plenty?
    - What surprises or disturbs you about the parable?
    - What do you think is the point of this parable?
4. Create a "Top Ten Reasons" chart.
    - Divide the whiteboard or a piece of chart paper into two columns headed "Not Prepared" and "Prepared."

- Ask the class to tell you the reasons that the bridesmaids might give for having just enough oil and the reasons for having more than enough oil. Write the answers on the chart.
- Mention the point that Pam Driedger makes about each group of bridesmaids exhibiting a kind of "faith"—one which waits to be in the middle of the crisis for God to intervene, and the other that prepares ahead of time. *Option:* If the group has more than 10 people, do this activity in small groups.

Integrate (15–20 minutes)

1. Ask:
    - How does the parable relate to the challenge of being prepared for a disaster or other crisis?
    - Based on the lists we just made, what are the reasons to prepare in advance for a crisis? What are the reasons you would just "take it with faith as it comes"?
    - What's the difference between preparing because we are afraid and preparing because we have faith in God?
    - What kind of crisis are you most afraid of? Do you want to prepare for it or just ignore it and hope it won't happen?
2. Activity
    - Ask each person to cut a piece of rope at least one foot long.
    - After everyone has a piece of rope, invite each person to tell the group what got them through the "horrible awful no good very bad day" they mentioned earlier. Ask them to tie a knot at the end of the rope when they are finished speaking.
    - When everyone has shared, write this on the whiteboard: *When you come to the end of your rope, tie a knot and hang on.*
    - Talk about the "knots" that they tied when they had bad days. How was God faithful to them? What helped

them to face their fears in the situation? What did they learn that will help them to face future bad days and crises? [Don't force this sharing; students may not have made a Christian commitment and/or have not experienced God's intervention on their bad days.]

- Say: *When we trust that God is present in all of life's circumstances we will know that God is also with us in times of deep crisis. Whether your "bad day" was a small or big crisis, and whether or not it was really a life-changing sad time, God was with you and will always be with you.*

  Jesus' parable of the bridesmaids challenges us to be prepared for the unexpected, and to depend on God when the unexpected bad things do happen.

  If you have time discuss the following questions. If not, ask them rhetorically for their reflection:

  - If there was a major crisis or disaster, what would you need from God?
  - From your parents and other adults?
  - From the church?
  - How can you be prepared in case something like this would happen?

Closing (5 minutes)

- Sing or read the words to the hymn "When peace, like a river" by Horatio Spafford. Offer this explanation: *This hymn was written by Horatio G. Spafford in 1876. He lost his real estate fortune in the Chicago fire of 1871. In 1873 four daughters died in a shipwreck, and in 1880 his son died of scarlet fever. Through the pain and sorrow, he penned the words, "It is well with my soul."*
- Invite youth to take their ropes home and to recall the words "It is well with my soul" when they look at the knot. Encourage them to hold the rope during their prayer time for the next week, using it to center their thoughts on God's faithfulness, which sees us through our fears.

2

Compassion Overcomes Blame

Neither this man nor his parents sinned; he was born blind so that God's works might be revealed in him.—John 9:3

It is natural for us to ask who or what is responsible for a crisis. The Scriptures, however, call us to focus on the opportunities we have to show God's grace and compassion, regardless of who is at fault.

Story: Nothando and her friend Abeni find their lives turned upside down by the AIDS epidemic in Zimbabwe, southern Africa. Despite the prejudices and fears of their family and friends, they choose to care for those who are suffering, regardless of their background.

Bible text: John 9:1-34—The man born blind

Supplies

- Bibles
- Video camera and equipment to show the video
- Someone to video tape the scene
- Pillar candle (optional closing)

Advance preparation

1. Read through the entire session, including the participant book.
2. Take time to read and reflect on the Bible story for the session.
3. Prepare a list of questions for the reporter in "Reflect on the Scripture."

4. Print the Teresa of Avila prayer (p. 51) on newsprint or whiteboard.

Opening (10 minutes)

Welcome and Focusing Activity

1. After all have arrived and you have welcomed them, go around the group and ask each student to say whether they are an "artist" or an "athlete." (They must choose one.)

2. Have the group count off by 3's (1,2,3...1,2,3...) In each group, the person whose name is closest to the letter A is the sculptor. The sculptor forms the other group members into a symbol that goes with the word that is assigned to them.

   Group 1 *Fear*

   Group 2 "*It's your fault*"

   Group 3 *Compassion*

3. When the groups are finished with their "sculpture," ask them to remember their positions. Then have each group present their sculture to the rest of the group.

Option: If the group is larger than 12 people, divide into six groups, with two groups per word.

Reflect on the story (10–12 minutes)

Read or tell the story, "Choosing to Love" (page 15 of *Beyond our Fears*). As they hear the story, they should try to imagine what they would do if they were in that person's shoes. After the story, discuss:

- How do you feel about what Nothando did? Was it the right choice?
- What would you have done if you were in her shoes?
- How do you feel about what Abeni did? Was it the right choice?
- What would you have done if you were in her shoes?

- Are some people more deserving of care than others? Why or why not?
- How were the women channels of God's peace?

Reflect on the Scripture text (15–20 minutes)

1. Ask for volunteers or assign the following parts:
   - Investigative reporter—needs to read John 9:1-34 and come up with questions to get to the bottom of what is going on.
   - Blind man
   - Jesus
   - Parent
   - Pharisees
   - Disciples
   - Jews
2. Have the entire group read the story. People with assigned roles should pay special attention to their character's actions and responses.
3. When everyone is familiar with their part of the story, the reporter goes "live" and asks questions to try to find out what happened.

   Examples of the reporter's questions:
   - What's going on here?
   - What did Jesus ask you to do?
   - And the mud did WHAT?
   - Parents, what do you know about this?
4. View the video and discuss:
   - Why do you think it was so important to the Pharisees that someone took the blame for the man's blindness?
   - With which of the characters in this story do you identify? Explain why.
   - What was Jesus' message about suffering?

Integrate (15–20 minutes)

1. Ponder and discuss.

   Say: *Jesus' disciples looked for a reason that would explain why God would make someone blind. The human desire to find a reason for suffering is not new. If we can find a reason we can explain the suffering and make it seem just. Jesus invites his followers to look at suffering in a new way—one which focuses on the opportunities to show compassion to those who suffer, no matter what the reason.*

   Discuss in pairs:

   - What connections do you see between the Scripture and the story about Nothando and Abeni?
   - Who are the people in your schools and neighborhood who need to experience God's grace and compassion?
   - How are you showing compassion? How does your congregation show compassion? How might these stories help you relate to a flu pandemic?
   - Is it wise or foolish for Christians to place themselves in harm's way in order to help the needy?

2. Prepare to be faithful.

   Share the following: *The HIV/AIDS epidemic in Zimbabwe and other parts of Africa may seem too distant to be a big concern for us. We can feel compassion for those who suffer or donate money to AIDS awareness and programs, but it doesn't seem to affect us right here. But we can imagine a flu pandemic where people around us are becoming sick and/or dying. Listen to the following warning from the Canadian government* [in the U.S., indicate that similar warnings come from the U.S. government as well]:

   > A pandemic is a worldwide outbreak of a specific disease which affects a large proportion of the population. There is no influenza pandemic activity anywhere in the world at this time, but scientists agree there will be a global outbreak of influenza (flu) sooner or later ...

It is very difficult to predict the impact of a pandemic, since no one knows how the virus would behave or how serious the pandemic would be. During a severe flu season, as many as 8,000 Canadians die from influenza and its complications; on average there are 4,000 deaths from annual flu. In a moderately severe pandemic, it is estimated that between 11,000 and 58,000 deaths may occur in Canada. These numbers are based on an assumption that the virus would cause illness in 15 to 35 per cent of the population.

In addition to deaths, a pandemic may cause significant illness and social disruption. It is important for Canadian families to plan ahead for a pandemic, because services provided by hospitals and clinics may be reduced or unavailable. Also, grocery stores and pharmacies may have limited supplies and banks may close.*

4. Refer to the Mennonite Church Canada Pandemic Resources website to find suggestions on how to be a caring faith community. If you are set up to go online in class, do so briefly. Go to www.churchpandemicresources.ca. Go to the section on how to prepare. Pay particular attention to the page which discusses caring before a pandemic. Identify some steps that you might take individually and/or as a congregation to prepare to extend healing and hope to people who are particularly vulnerable.

   Discuss:

   - How do we prepare ourselves to act with the same compassion we witnessed in today's stories?
   - How do we prepare ourselves to be the hands of Jesus during a major health disaster?

---

* www.hc-sc.gc.ca/hl-vs/iyh-vsv/diseases-maladies/pandem-eng.php (The U.S. government website www.pandemicflu.gov/index.html contains similar information.) See the FAQ section under pandemic influenza.

Closing (5 minutes)

Say: *In the skit some of you portrayed different roles. We are all different—based on our talents, our ethnicity, our culture, our financial resources, our skills, our interests, our backgrounds and experiences. We are very different! But Jesus calls each one of us to be caring people. Jesus doesn't care if you're a math whiz or a mechanic, a computer geek or a running back. Jesus cares that you care! Everybody can share compassion with somebody else—now or in a time of crisis. We can trust that God will walk with us and strengthen and encourage us as we become the presence of Christ to others.*

So, let's stand in a circle and read this blessing together:

Christ has no body now on earth but yours;

Yours are the only hands with which Christ can do his work [lift hands],

Yours are the only feet with which Christ can go about the world [point to feet],

Yours are the only eyes through which Christ's compassion [put hands next to eyes]

can shine forth upon a troubled world [raise hands up and out to sides].

Christ has no body on earth now but yours [join hands in the circle].

3

Service Overcomes Self-Preservation

Let each of you look not to your own interests, but to the interests of others. Let the same mind be in you that was in Christ Jesus . . .—Philippians 2:4-7

Our human reaction is to escape or to build walls of protection around ourselves when our health or safety is threatened. God calls us to be prudent, but also to follow Jesus, who gave his own life in service to others.

Story: A strange disease, SARS, threatens to spread throughout Toronto in the spring of 2003. Amanda, a nurse, must wear protective clothing at work, and is quarantined at home. But she knows that she is doing what God has called her to do: care for sick people, no matter what the personal risks.

Bible text: Philippians 2:1-11—God comes as a human servant

Supplies

- Recording of the song, "Here I am, Lord" (text and music by Daniel Schutte and New Dawn Music, 1981) and player, OR hymnals to sing this or a different song of commitment to service
- Copies of Philippians 2:1-11 from *The Message* translation, one per student
- Flip chart and markers OR masking tape for Integrate activity
- Inexpensive dust masks—one per student and leader (recycle or re-use later)
- Inexpensive latex gloves—one set per student and teacher (recycle or re-use later)

Advance preparation

1. Read through the entire session, including the participant book.

2. Take time to read and reflect on the Bible story for this session.

3. Create a Venn diagram on the Flip chart/white board OR on the floor with tape. Draw two large circles that overlap in the center. Print these headings: "Practical Human Wisdom" (left) and "The Mind of Christ" (right), and "The Best of Both" (center). If you do the circles on the floor, print the words on paper and lay them inside the circles.

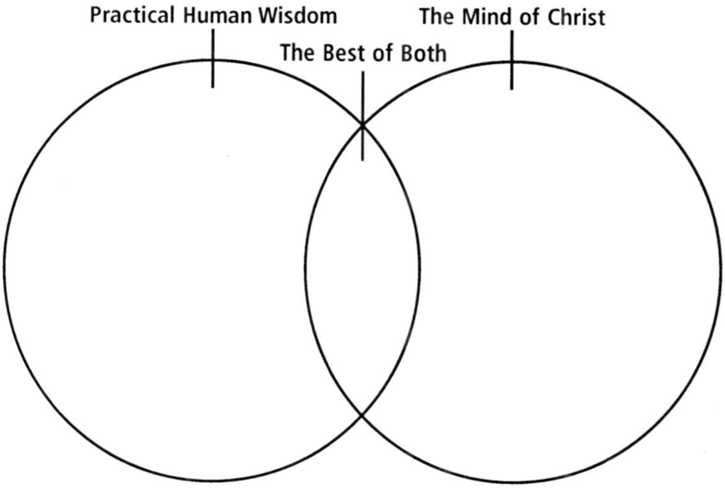

Opening (10 minutes)

Welcome and Focusing Activity

1. Welcome students and hand them a dust mask as they arrive. Begin the session by asking if they have done anything risky during the past week, and if so, what. Note that some people might share activities that are dangerous or even illegal. Don't respond at this time. Keep going around the circle. If you want to address the behavior wait until after class or at another time.

2. Say: *People wear masks to protect themselves from disease, dust, and pollution, to minimize risk.*

3. Ask:

    - How much of a risk taker are you? If not at all, put your mask on your face. If you love to take risks, put the mask on your lap. If you take some risks, wear the mask around your neck.
    - How willing would you be to donate a kidney to a close relative or friend? If you would not do it, put mask on face. If you would, put the mask on your lap.
    - If you were caught in the middle of a dangerous situation (say, violence or a pandemic) would you risk your life in order to save a stranger's life? If no, put the mask on. If yes, put it on your lap.
    - If a good friend of yours had AIDS but was doing well, would you go on a potentially dangerous rafting trip with him or her? If no, put the mask on. If yes, put it on your lap.

4. Discuss responses. Was it hard to know how to respond? If so, what made it hard?
5. Say: *Our theme today is "Service Overcomes Self-Preservation." The desire to preserve our own lives is strong, but it isn't always the way of Jesus.*

Reflect on the story (10 minutes)

1. Ask youth to close their eyes and imagine they are Amanda and Johanna while you read or tell the story from "Choosing to Serve" (*Beyond our Fears*, page 21).
2. Go around the room and invite students to give one-word responses that describe how they felt as they heard the story. Then discuss the following:
    - What motivated Amanda and Johanna to take those risks?
    - What role did the faith community play in their decisions?
    - What role did family members play in the decisions?
    - If you were a relative or close friend of a healthcare provider in this situation, how would you respond?

Reflect on the Scripture text (10 minutes)

1. Hand out the gloves and ask the group to put them on. Then hand out the Philippians 2:1-11 passage and read it together. Ask the group to think about how wearing the gloves does or doesn't fit with what they are reading in the passage. After you've read it, discuss:

    - How does the symbol of gloves relate to the passage we read? (Look at verse 7 especially. Are there two meanings here—take off the gloves and help people, or put them on to be safe while helping people?)

    - What does it mean to have the mind of Christ?

2. Say: *In today's society we are often encouraged to take care of ourselves first. Large organizations devote a lot of time to the issue of risk reduction. Mainstream society tends to view anyone who is willing to die for his or her faith as a fanatic. So how do we understand the call of Philippians 2, which encourages us to be like Christ Jesus—willing to risk our lives for the sake of others? Are we really supposed to do that? Or is that call just for super-Christians?*

youth guide

Integrate (15–20 minutes)

Ponder and discuss.

1. Fill out the Venn diagram together. On the left, write reasons that "the world" would give for choosing not to risk one's life in service during a pandemic (e.g., I have a lot of living to do; I'm afraid to die; I take care of myself—why shouldn't others?).

2. On the right, write reasons that Christians who have the mind of Christ would give for choosing to risk their lives (e.g., show the love of God; strengthen my faith in God).

3. In the overlapping space, write motivations that reflect both worldly and Christian views (e.g., helping others helps the whole community).

    Discuss:

    - Who should be expected to care for the sick during a

pandemic or highly contagious epidemic? Should Christians be expected to take more risks?

- What fears must we face if we are willing to serve God faithfully in such a crisis?

Prepare to be faithful.

1. Read or summarize the account of how the choices made by early Christians during the epidemic as noted in the Scripture reflection (*Beyond our Fears* page 25 and the story of Bishop Cyprian, page 33). Ask: as a result of the Christians' willingness to risk their lives at this time, people took notice and the church grew. How did they get the courage to do that? Would we do the same?

2. Say: *Let's imagine that a new flu virus is spreading rapidly through North America in pandemic proportions. There have been no cases in your community, but a hospital in a nearby city has had an unusually high number of cases. Many of the staff have also been infected. The hospital has sent out a request to health professionals in neighboring areas asking them to come and help. Two nurses and two doctors—parents of youth in your youth group—are thinking about going. They are asking your congregation to help them discern if they should go. What do you think? What if one of them was your parent?*

3. Discuss the above scenario briefly, and then move on to this one:

   Imagine that our youth group is looking for places to go for a summer service trip. One option is an area that has just experienced severe flooding. There have been some health issues there due to the results of the flood. In general, if people are careful, there shouldn't be any problems, but there are some risks. Should your youth group go?

   Divide into pairs, come to a decision, and then share with the larger group.

Closing (5 minutes)

Ask the group to join you in putting on the masks and gloves. Form a circle. Ask everyone to follow your actions as you all sing or listen to the song "Here I am, Lord" (or the alternative song that opened your session). For the first verse, hold your hands up in front of you. When the chorus begins, slowly remove your gloves and then the mask. Then stretch your arms out in front of you. When the song ends, join hands and say this prayer:

> *May Jesus, who gave his life for us, give us the courage to take risks for the sake of others. Amen.*

4

Living in Hope Overcomes Darkness

youth guide

If you . . . satisfy the needs of the afflicted, then your light shall rise in the darkness and your gloom be like the noonday.—Isaiah 58:10

The light of God will shine in the darkness of any crisis as the church participates faithfully and courageously in God's restoring work.

Story: In 1666, two local church leaders convince the people of Eyam, England, to voluntarily quarantine their village to keep the bubonic plague from spreading to neighboring communities. Today, the village is still remembered as a beacon of sacrificial love.

Bible text: Isaiah 58:6-12—God's promise of restoration

Supplies

- Copies of the *The Message* for the Scripture reading
- Pillar candle
- Small tea lights or floating candles (opening)
- Large glass bowl, large enough to hold the pillar candle and a tea light for each person
- Water
- Book of matches or a lighter
- Flip chart, markers
- Newsprint, markers
- Lego™ bricks or similar toy "building" material
- Small flashlights, one for each student

Advance preparation

1. Read through the entire session, including the participant book.

2. Fill the bowl with water and place the pillar candle in the middle of it. Set it in a visible accessible place. Place matches and tea lights around the bowl.

3. Ask someone in the group (or a visitor, if appropriate) to prepare to tell the story "A Village Quarantines Itself" (page 28 of *Beyond our Fears*) in a dramatic fashion.

4. Divide the white board or chart paper into two columns. On one column write *Our Actions*; on the other, *God's Promises.*

Opening (10 minutes)

1. Welcome students as they gather. Dim the lights if you can. Gather the students in a circle around the pillar candle and tea lights.

2. Say: *For the last three sessions, we've been talking about how Christians are called to respond to crises such as disasters and pandemics. This topic can cast a shadow over us as we think of such situations and their effects on our families and our community. As Christians, however, we have the assurance that God cares and is present in dark times. We light this Christ candle as a symbol of that presence.* [Light the pillar candle.] *To live in hope and faith means to take risks and to face the future knowing that God will sustain us. As a way to express our desire to be faithful to God, I invite you to light a tea light candle and place it in the bowl of water.* [Students light the tea candles.] *See, as more candles are lit, there is less darkness. Each of us can indeed be vessels through which Christ's light shines into the world.*

3. Turn on the lights but leave the candles burning.

Reflect on the story (15–20 minutes)

Listen to the story of Eyam as shared by the person you invited to tell it.

1. Say: *I want you to think about this story and reflect your thoughts, feelings, and questions through your choice of several mediums:*
   - newsprint and markers to create an illustration or write a poem or paragraph of thoughts.
   - Legos™ to create something symbolic of your thoughts
   - a short song that you write to express your thoughts (may use a tune that you know)
2. Ask students to describe their creations and tell how they relate to the story.
3. Discuss:
   - Why do you think the villagers responded as they did?
   - Does this sacrifice inspire you? Why or why not?
   - Do you think that the actions of the villagers could be replicated 400 years later in our own community? Why or Why not?

Reflect on the Scripture text (10 minutes)

1. Before reading Isaiah 58: 6-12 from *The Message*, ask the group to listen carefully to the text and be prepared to say "light" when they hear what actions of the people bring light into the darkness, and "promise" when they hear a promise from God. On a flip chart, list the "light" and "promises" as you slowly read the passage to the group.
2. Divide into smaller groups or pairs and ask them to consider the Scripture text in light of a disease pandemic. Ask them to think of several specific actions that they could take that would bring God's light into the darkness of a pandemic. For each action, consider a promise that God has given that would bring hope to the caregivers. These can be added to the lists on the flip chart.

3. *Option:* Create a litany out of this assignment. Have the pairs write their actions and promises into "If-then" sentences, similar to the biblical verses. Example: *If you invite a homeless person to lunch with you, then God's light will shine in the darkness.* Each pair will contribute to the litany.

Integrate (15–20 minutes)

1. Ponder and discuss.

   Say: *The stories and Scripture we have heard in this series suggest that the church and God's people can bring light in the darkness through our acts of compassion and courage in the face of a crisis. When we move beyond our fears and trust that God will light our way, we can offer hope to a world that is falling apart. The stories we've heard tell of real people who chose to bring light in the midst of despair, because of their Christian convictions.*

   - How have these stories inspired you?
   - What did you learn from this study that has strengthened your faith?
   - What fears do you still feel about crises?
   - Does awareness about a pandemic increase or decrease your fears and/or your faith?
   - How can your congregation or youth group apply the lessons from these stories?

2. Prepare to be faithful.

   Assign the following scenarios to small groups to discuss and report back to the whole group.

   Scenario #1: Your best friend's father is diagnosed with a new bird flu that is highly contagious and for which there is no reliable treatment. Your friend calls to say she is running a fever and feeling weak; she needs someone to babysit her little sister while her mother's at work. The little sister doesn't have any symptoms. Will you go?

   Scenario #2: Your mother is the chaplain at a local hospital. The hospital has had numerous cases of the pandemic flu that is devastating the country. So far the flu has been contained to four hospital wards. Because spiritual care is not considered an essential service, your mom is given a choice to work on these wards or stay at home. If she chooses to work there, she will need to go into be quarantined. What should she do?

Scenario #3: A pandemic flu is spreading throughout the country. Many homeless shelters have shut down and soup kitchens have closed because there are not enough volunteers. More than a dozen people have called your church in the past week looking for food and a place to stay. Several are coughing or wheezing. A congregational meeting has been called to discuss what your church can do. You are on the church council. What would you recommend?

Scenario #4: Make up a scenario that is specific to your congregation and the members of your group. Who would be particularly vulnerable during a time of crisis? How can you serve them?

Closing (5 minutes)

1. Dim the lights again. Hand out the small flashlights.

   Pray: *Our prayer, O God, is that we will be faithful in times of crisis. We want to be ready to stand for hope in the midst of despair. We want to be your light in the shadows.*

2. Ask the youth to turn on their flashlights and sing "This Little Light of Mine."

   Say: *Take this light home. Keep it as a reminder that you are a light in this world. God uses you to spread light where there is darkness. May you go in God's peace and God's strength.*

Children's Activities

To use with *Don't Be Afraid*

The following activity suggestions are coordinated with the four stories of *Don't Be Afraid: Stories of Christians in Times of Trouble* by Rebecca Seiling and Cindy Snider. They are intended for children ages 9 to 12, and can be used in mid-week club settings, intergenerational small groups, or part of the opening time before Sunday school.

If your congregation is planning a series on crisis preparedness, a note at the end of each section explains connections to the book for adults and youth: *Beyond our Fears: Following Jesus During Times of Crisis*, for which outlines are included in this leader's guide (see pages 11 and 39).

Stories 1, 2, and 4 in *Don't Be Afraid* are fictionalized accounts based on the true life stories you will read in *Beyond our Fears*. Story 3 is a based on the history of the church's response to the plagues of the third century; it is included as an appendix in *Beyond our Fears*.

In your planning, read the story before selecting which activities will work best with your children, the time available, and the setting. If you plan to use these stories with younger children, be sure to adapt the activities appropriately.

We recommend that each child or family has a copy of *Don't Be Afraid*. Children can read the stories again and again to remind them that God is with them in times of trouble.

For each story, you will find a variety of ways to explore the themes. When you have made your selections, gather supplies, set up your learning space, and prepare you teaching plan.

Story 1

The House that Love Built

Background

Bible key: Don't let anyone look down on you because you are young. Set an example ... in what you say and in how you live. Also set an example in how you love and in what you believe.—*1 Timothy 4:12 (New International Reader's Version)*

Story summary: The storyteller of *The House that Love Built* was twelve years old. Mike didn't let his age, however, keep him from helping his family in the aftermath of Hurricane Katrina. He responded to a scary situation by focusing on God's love and care. He encouraged his mother when she was full of worry, and he persisted in his faith that God loved them and would take care of them.

Faith connection: Children and young people are important in God's plan for the world. Jesus was twelve when he went to the temple in Jerusalem and visited with the teachers. He listened to them and asked them questions. Everyone who heard Jesus talk was amazed at his understanding and his answers to the adults' questions. No doubt Jesus was very familiar with God's Word.

In this story, Mike was able to trust in God by relying on God's Word and focusing on God's love. Perhaps he even felt God's presence as he walked through that smelly mud. He had faith that things would get better with God's help—and they did!

Children can encourage adults to trust in God's faithful presence. They can use their gifts of compassion and encouragement in times of crises.

Activity Suggestions

1. Read the story

If children have their own books, have them turn to the first story and look at the pictures. Invite them to tell of a time when they were in a big storm. Were they afraid? What did they do about their fear?

Depending on the reading capabilities of the group, determine how the story will be read. You can read it well and have them listen or follow along. Or read it using several voices to read the narration, Mike's words, and Mike's mother's words. Or have a few good readers read sections of the story at a time.

2. Talk

- What surprised you about the story?
- If you were Mike, how might you have responded when your house was destroyed?
- Can you remember a time when you were scared, but you were still able to trust in God?
- Can you remember a time when you let fear get the best of you?
- Do you feel confident that God can use you to help others, even though you are young?

Connections with *Beyond our Fears*

This story is based on the true account told in Chapter 1 of *Beyond our Fears*, but adds a fictional point of view of Carmen's 12-year-old son. The faith focus of *Beyond our Fears* is the connections between faith and preparedness; here, it is about the gifts that young people can bring to a crisis situation.

3. Sing

Sing or listen to all the verses of "Will you let me be your servant" (Richard Gillard). Ask: *Which verse do you think relates most to Mike's story?* Make motions to go with the phrases in the first verse. Listen to or sing the first verse again using the motions.

4. Bible key and prayer

Read the Bible key verse. Use a talking stick or flashlight to guide the conversation. The person holding the stick will complete the sentence: "Even though I'm young, I can still ..." or tell a story of a time you encouraged an adult.

Invite someone to read this prayer:

> God, sometimes I wonder what I can do to help in difficult situations, since I'm not an adult. But the story of Mike reminds me that you work through younger people to bring hope to others, including the adults in our lives. Give me the courage I need to act and speak deeds and words of love today. Amen.

5. Build a wall

Attach large pieces of white poster board to the wall or to a wooden frame. Have the children write their names and the names of friends and family on the new wall. Add some favorite Bible verses. Each week add the Bible key to the wall.

6. Do a word search

Distribute pencils and copies of the word search (included on page 69). Children will search for 54 words that appeared in the story, "The House that Love Built."

7. Take action

It's good to be prepared, to practice, and to think about what we would do in a disaster, crisis, or emergency. Make a list of things families can do to prepare for a natural disaster. Make a list of things the church can do in times of a disaster. Give this list to your church leaders.

Meanwhile, think of ways to help people in your community who are having a rough time because of illness, job loss, or other crises. Encourage children and families to do a volunteer service activity in their community, such as volunteer at the soup kitchen, take a meal to a new neighbor, or a senior who is not able to cook.

8. Research

Check out the website for Mennonite Disaster Service to learn about the people and places that were helped in times of natural disasters. MDS was actively involved in rebuilding homes damaged or destroyed during Hurricane Katrina. Go to: www.mds.mennonite.net

The House that Love Built

Word Search

s g r o s s h e t c r l g c k g g a
m s l i m y m m i h a p e c o s a r
s i r b e d l i u b e r a u c d t s
e s u o h b u l l d o z e r u u r t
h t i a f g n i n e t s i l e e u o
o e i a a n n y l d b p t n y n s r
g r a n d p a r e n t s c a k i t y
r c g s o g i p w u l o r o g c n s
o e h p o n u t r o u p h l o a u g
o s t u h i n e v r r c s o d l a m
v g i - r y t e a r r k p v w i n d
e n t n o r f g m u s l i i e t o y
k i e w b c i t h s e l c n u o o u
n h e o h n x c g h c o l g g u o c
s g r r g n i m a e r c s a n t u k
s u t g i o t h a n k i n g w i e y
b a s k e t b a l l e t t e r s a e
o l v g n i k s a c a m t n m i o r

hurricane
scripture
care
wind
street
house
story
fix
debris
loving
cool

groove
God
aunts
young
yucky
prayers
neighborhood
parents
bulldozer
muck
crying

letters
Mennonite
grandparents
laughing
basketball
listening
secret
uncles
encouraging
gross
mud

thanking
church
surrounded
relying
wet
faith
working
help
grown-ups
walls
asking

adults
love
good
slimy
screaming
rebuild
trust
sister
smile
rain

Story 2

You Are God's Hands

Background

Bible key: Once, when [Jesus] was in one of the cities, there was a man covered with leprosy. When he saw Jesus, he bowed with his face to the ground and begged him, "Lord, if you choose, you can make me clean." Then Jesus stretched out his hand, touched him, and said, "I do choose. Be made clean." Immediately the leprosy left him.—*Luke 5:12-13*

Story summary: The AIDS epidemic has swept through the continent of Africa, devastating families and communities. Some people think that having a disease like AIDS is God's punishment for people's bad behavior, so we shouldn't have to help them. But we know that God wants us to serve everyone, no matter what they have done. Jesus calls us to stop "putting on the blame" and devote our energy, instead, to making things better.

In biblical times the word "leprosy" was used for many different kinds of skin diseases. Sometimes the disease was so bad that it ate away a person's face. Jesus healed many people including those with skin diseases. Just as people with AIDS today are often treated as outcasts, people with leprosy were sent away to live by themselves. Nobody wanted to see them or touch them. Jesus, on the other hand, willingly touched them and helped them to become well.

Faith Connection: Children can learn how to be compassionate with people who are sick. They can share Jesus' love by using their hands to help make things better for others.

Activity Suggestions

1. Read the story

Invite a woman to read or tell this story. Consider bringing simple props to help tell the story. Encourage the children to imagine being in the story and the senses that they experience.

2. Talk

- What about the story surprised you?
- What advice would you have given this woman if she was your mom?
- What senses were involved as you imagine the scenes from this story?
- What do you see in your mind? Describe it.
- What do you hear?
- What do you smell? Is there any food cooking? Any medicine smells?
- How many touches in the story?
- Was the sense of taste included in the story?

Connections with *Beyond our Fears*

This story is based on the true account told in Chapter 2 of *Beyond our Fears*, but adds the fictional element of Amy's perspective. The faith focus of study in *Beyond our Fears* is the call to serve people who suffer, rather than blaming them. Here, it is about reaching out to those in need, allowing our hands to be the hands of God.

3. Research leprosy

Check out Bible dictionaries or commentaries to learn more about leprosy. Read two stories from the Bible that tell how Jesus treated people with skin diseases. Read Luke 5:12-16 and Luke 17:11-19. Make a chart that gives a definition of leprosy, a description of what it looks like, how it was treated, and what Jesus taught us about relating to people with leprosy.

4. Research AIDS

Check out dictionaries and medical journals or websites to learn more about AIDS/HIV. Complete a chart similar to the one suggested above.

5. Bible key and prayer

Read the Bible key. Talk about the fact that not everyone is healed from sickness. Does that mean God doesn't care about them? Remind children that when people become sick with diseases, it is not punishment from God. God is with them in their suffering.

Pray: *God, we don't understand why sickness and suffering happen. We wonder, why don't you do something? People need you to heal them!* [pause] *God, maybe this is your way of telling us to reach out to those who are sick and sad and discouraged because of their illness. Help us to be willing to use our hands and bodies to touch others with your love. Amen.*

Sing. You may have heard someone say that "Jesus can use our hands and feet today." Can God use your hands and feet? If you have access to Matt Maher's recording Empty and Beautiful, play and sing along with the song. "Shine Like the Son." (The CD can be purchased and a preview listen is available on the internet at: http://www.spiritandsong.com/artists/mattmaher)

Are there other songs that the children know that express the sentiment that children can serve God in practical ways by showing care and compassion for those who are sick.

6. Sculpt soap carvings

In Zimbabwe, which means "house of stone," sculptors from the Shona tribal group carve remarkable sculptures from stone. Stone carving requires special tools and weeks of work, but soap carving is pretty easy. Here's what you'll need: bars of soap (Ivory works best for carving), butter knives, potato peelers, nails, and plastic tablecloth or covering.

Prepare a work space and distribute bars of soap, one per person. Use a knife and potato peeler to carve an image. Use a nail to make eyes, and use your imagination to add texture, etc. Give children ideas on what to carve before they begin. *Suggestions*: a cross, an African animal, a person's face. The soap sculpture can be a reminder how Nothando showed compassion to patients with AIDS in Africa. As children carve, talk about ways they can help people with AIDS now. (Avoid wasting any soap by moistening your soap scraps and squeezing them together into a soap ball.)

7. Make AIDS care kits.

You can take action now by helping your church collect items for AIDS Care Kits for Mennonite Central Committee. Each kit contains items that can be used by people like Nothando who provide home-based care to people living with AIDS. Please collect only new items. The items to collect include the following:

- 1 bar bath soap (90-140 g/ 4-5 oz; in wrapper)
- 1 bath towel (medium weight, bright color)
- 1 washcloth (bright color)
- 2 flat bedsheets (twin size)
- 2 pillowcases (standard size)
- 2 yards fabric (poly-cotton, bright color)
- 1 pair rubber gloves (large size; for household cleaning)
- 1 container petroleum jelly (approx. 368 g/13 oz; sealed in plastic bag)
- 1 container of medicated body powder (i.e. Gold Bond; approx. 283 g/10 oz)
- $100 to purchase medicines and Bibles for people living with AIDS and to train volunteers in basic home health-care. Make check payable to "MCC—AIDS Care Kit."

Place all your items and your check in a drawstring shoulder bag. Find your nearest MCC kit collection center online at www.mcc.org/aids/kits, or call your regional MCC office.

Story 3

No One Will Be Abandoned

Background

Bible key: I was hungry, and you gave me food. I was thirsty and you gave me something to drink. I was a stranger and you welcomed me. I was naked and you gave me clothing. I was sick and you took care of me. I was in prison and you visited me.—*Matthew 25:35-36*

Story Summary: In the first centuries of the church, Christianity was not a popular faith. The Roman government and people who were not Christians treated Christians harshly—sometimes putting them in prison and even killing them. So how did the church grow so much? One reason was that Christian believers took seriously Jesus' words about showing love to everyone, including enemies. In Matthew 25:31-46 Jesus encourages his followers to show compassion toward "the least of these"—people who are hungry, thirsty, strangers, naked, sick, and imprisoned. Jesus says that by caring for these people, we care for Jesus himself.

As the story of Cyprian shows, Christians became known for caring for people in the times of the plagues—even if those people had persecuted the Christians, and even if it meant putting their own lives at risk. This kind of love attracted others to the way of Jesus, and the church grew.

Faith Connection: Children learn that caring for others, especially in times of danger, is one way to express our love for Jesus.

Activity Suggestions

1. Read the story

Find a creative way to read or tell this story. Ask the children to imagine living at a time of spreading disease and when there is no modern medicine and hospitals to serve the sick.

2. Talk

- What surprised you in this story?
- What made Bishop Cyprian help the sick man on the street?
- If you had been part of his church, what would have gone through your mind?
- What made the church member come together and risk their lives to help even the people who had persecuted them?
- When might you have seen the face of Jesus in someone you helped?

3. Sing

Choose songs about God's help in times of suffering. Instead of singing the songs, read the words and/or listen to recorded versions of them.

4. Bible key and prayer

Read the Bible key. Think about being the one who receives care from someone. Draw or find pictures that illustrate this verse.

Pray:

When will we see your face, God?
In the hungry?
In the thirsty?
In the stranger at my door?
In the sick?
In the prisoner?
When will we see your face, God?

Connections with *Beyond our Fears*

This story, included as an appendix in *Beyond our Fears*, is a fictionalized account based on the true story of Bishop Cyprian of the third century. The witness of the third-century church during the time of the plagues is mentioned in Chapter 3 in *Beyond our Fears*. In *Don't Be Afraid*, the story brings out one key part of that witness: helping even enemies.

The story for Chapter 3 in *Beyond our Fears* is the basis of the fourth (and next) story in *Don't Be Afraid*, about the SARS crisis. In Chapter 4 of *Beyond our Fears*, the story is another historical one: of how a village in England confronted the plague in the 17th century. An additional activity for this session might be to retell that story to your group.

Open our eyes to see.
Open our hands to serve.
Show your face to us—just a glimpse—
So that we know we are serving you.
Amen.

5. **Run an obstacle course**

The church in Carthage worked hard to care for people who were sick and dying. Use props and act out the various jobs that people did to help. Pretend you are helping to rescue sick people from the streets. Set up an obstacle course and have a small group run a relay. Two people carry a friend through the obstacle course, and back again. This continues until each person has had a turn to carry or to be carried. By carrying people physically, you can pretend that you are carrying their burdens, or the things that are bothering them.

6. **Make a collage**

Some people imagine that God's face looks like all the people's faces mixed together. Find faces in magazines to cut and paste, and cover a piece of poster board with different faces. Post this "glimpse of God" on the bulletin board.

7. **Make health kits.**

Collect items to make health kits for Mennonite Central Committee, to be sent to areas where people need relief. See www.mcc.org or call you nearest MCC office for fuller instructions. Each kit requires the following new items:

- 1 toothbrush (adult size; leave in wrapper)
- 1 squeeze-tube toothpaste (minimum 130ml / 6oz; leave in box)
- 1 large bar of bath soap
- 1 fingernail clipper
- 1 hand towel (larger than fingertip, dark color)

Health kits are distributed in a useful double drawstring cloth bag (28cm x 40.6cm / 11in x 16in). You may sew the bag yourself (instructions available through MCC) or request bags from an MCC collection center, or donate contents that MCC will place in a bag.

Drop off completed health kits at one of the drop-off locations in Canada or the U.S.

Story 4

Love Behind a Mask

Bible Background

Bible key: For God did not give us a spirit of cowardice, but rather a spirit of power and of love and of self-discipline. —*2 Timothy 1:7*

Story summary: There may be times when God prods us to take a leap of faith and to trust that God will be with us in risky situations. In this story Amanda took her nursing job seriously, confident that God would help her do the right thing. People around her—even her family—were fearful at first, but as they learned more about acting wisely during the SARS crisis, they too learned to relax and top trust.

Faith Connection: In times of trouble, it is easy to be afraid or nervous. We may prefer to run away, or to avoid doing the courageous thing. But when God calls us to reach out in times of need, God also promises to give us the power and the love we need.

Activity Suggestions

1. Read the story

Find a creative way to tell or read this story with the children.

2. Talk

- In this story, Amanda takes a risk by caring for the people she works with. She feels called by God to be a nurse. What would you have done in her shoes?
- Amanda and her family felt fearful about the SARS virus spreading to them. What do you do in times of fear? How does your faith help you to have courage?

- Can you imagine jumping in and serving others like Amanda did—being God's hands during a time of crisis? The world needs people like that. The world needs people of courage, people of love who will take risks to help others. How can you join in?

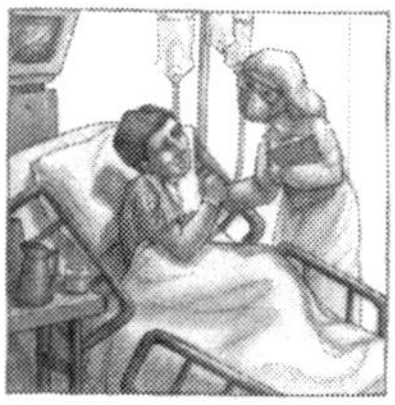

3. Sing

Sing or listen to songs about courage in the face of danger. Talk about the ways that music can calm us during times of trouble. Consider playing some quiet instrumental music while children sit quietly and draw or play with a piece of cloth or play dough.

4. Bible key and prayer

In 2 Timothy 1:7, the writer describes the spirit that God gives us: a spirit of "power and love and self-discipline." How is that spirit at work in you?

Pray the following prayer, inviting the children to repeat the couplets after you:

God of boldness, you give us courage.
(children repeat)

God of light, you give us hope.
(children repeat)

God of tenderness, you give us love.
(children repeat)

God of strength, you give us power.
(children repeat)

Thank you for giving us the courage to risk, hope to go on, love to embrace others, and power to heal our world. Amen.

Option: Assign four children to read the first four leader lines.

Connections with *Beyond our Fears*

This story is based on the true account told in Chapter 3 of *Beyond our Fears*, and focuses on overcoming our fears in order to do God's work in the world. The faith focus of *Beyond our Fears* Chapter 3 is about risk-taking, and the faith focus of Chapter 4 is about the church living with hope and courage as they join God's mission in the world, even in dark times.

5. Trust game

Practice your spirit of power, love and self-discipline as you attempt these tasks with a partner.

Trust walk: Partner A is blindfolded. It is Partner B's job to carefully guide Partner A around a space, using only verbal instructions. Be careful! Your partner trusts you to lead safely! You can try this with a group too. The group links arms while closing their eyes. A leader leads them safely around a big space.

Trust run: Partner A is blindfolded. In a large, open space, Partner B instructs Partner A to go from a walk to a run, and back to a walk. Make sure you run alongside your partner when you are leading!

6. Research

Check out websites about pandemics to learn about communicable diseases and what children can do to take care of themselves during an epidemic or flu outbreak. Encourage children to talk with their parents about the things they can do to prepare for an outbreak of an illness that spreads. The website associated with *Beyond our Fears* and *Don't Be Afraid* is: www.churchpandemicresources.ca

7. Interview

Invite someone who works in the medical field, or someone who cares for people who are terminally ill through a hospice program in your community. Ask them what keeps them going each day.

8. Collect toys

Call a local hospital to see what types of toys they could use in their children's ward. Collect toys to bring to your local hospital for children.

9. Make a card

If you know someone who is not well, make a card or a small craft. Visit with that person, and present your gift. Your presence with them will be the greatest present!

Congregational Prayers for Times of Crisis

The following prayers may be adapted freely for use in any worship settings that occur in the context of crisis. Additional resources are offered in the sample services found on pages 87-97. Worship resources can also be gleaned from the stories and Scripture reflections of the study book, *Beyond our Fears: Following Jesus in Times of Crisis*, and from the accompanying adult and youth leader guides included in this volume (pages 11 and 39).

Call to worship

(inspired by Psalm 137)

L: Come, let us worship God, who laughs and cries with us.
Let us praise the One whose suffering
encompasses the breadth of our pain,
and whose delight surpasses our deepest joy.

P: **We worship the God who knows our thoughts and feelings**
even before we name them.
We honor the One who welcomes our laments
as well as our songs of thanksgiving.

All: May all the words of our mouths
and the meditations of our hearts
be acceptable in your sight, O God. Amen.

By Karla Stoltzfus. From *Words for Worship 2* (Scottdale, PA and Waterloo, ON: Herald Press, 2009). Permission is granted to reprint this prayer for a single congregational use.

Gathering for a service of lament

L: In our weakest moments, through the darkest hours,
P: you walk with us.
L: In our moments of joy, through the brightest celebrations,
P: you walk with us.
L: In our abundance,
P: you walk with us.
L: In our poverty,
P: you walk with us.
L: To the cross,
P: you walk with us.
L: Even through death,
P: you walk with us.
L: Into new abundant life,
P: you walk with us.
L: Because we cannot do it alone,
P: you walk with us.
L: Lord, grant us grace to remember to follow. Amen.

By Jessica Schrock-Ringenberg. From *Words for Worship 2* (Scottdale, PA and Waterloo, ON: Herald Press, 2009).

Prayer in the wake of a disaster

(based on Mark 4:35-41)

Living God, our refuge and strength, even the wind and sea obey your voice. Put the wind back in its place, and say to the sea: Peace! Be still! Fill us with great faith, and save us from the surging water, so that we may tell the good news of your saving love; through Jesus Christ, our hope in the storm.

Holy One, you are our comfort and strength in times of sudden disaster, crisis, or chaos. By your Spirit, lift up those who have fallen, sustain those who work to rescue or rebuild, and fill us with the hope of your new creation.

Surround us now with your grace and peace. Guide our minds and hearts. Grant us wisdom and discernment, so that in all things we bring glory to your name.

In your Son's name we pray, Amen.

Confession for times of heightened fear and anxiety

(based on Isaiah 43)

L: Hear the word of the Lord:
"Fear not, for I have saved you;
I have called you by name; you are mine."

P: **God our Savior, we confess our fear,
which keeps us from fully loving our neighbors,
our enemies, and even you.
Call us by name and save us!**
(silence)

L: "When you pass through the waters, I will be with you;
and when you pass through the rivers,
they will not drown you."

P: **God our Keeper, the waters are getting higher.
Our jobs, families, finances, and responsibilities
overwhelm us.
The troubles of the world exhaust us.
We lift the sinful worry of these chaotic waters to you.
Pull us to dry land!**
(silence)

L: "When you walk through the fire, you will not be burned;
the flames will not set you ablaze."

P: **God our Protector, we confess
that we do not always fully trust you.
Instead, we trust our politics, our technology,
our entertainment, more than you.
Forgive our idolatry.**
(silence)

L: "Do not be afraid, for I the LORD God, am with you.
I love you. You are precious in my sight." Amen.

By Willmar T. Harder. From *Words for Worship 2* (Scottdale, PA and Waterloo, ON: Herald Press, 2009). Permission is granted to reprint this prayer for a single congregational use.

We wait in hope

(based on Psalm 130)

From the depths of our sadness
we cry out to you, merciful God:
hear us,
heal us,
strengthen us.
Show us how to be your people.
Teach us to walk in your ways, without fear.
Encourage us to build bridges and not walls,
to risk our lives for your reign.

Rock our complacency, mighty God.
Give us a vision of the New Jerusalem.
For you have surely walked with us in the past.
You have taught us and carried us to this place.

Therefore we sing of your love and mercy,
your justice and your shalom.
We proclaim your goodness as we wait in hope
for your love to cast out fear
and change our lives.

Then we will sing of your praises
by the riverbanks of our city.
Then we will acknowledge that you alone are God
forever and ever. Amen.

By Carmen Schrock-Hurst. From *Words for Worship 2* (Scottdale, PA and Waterloo, ON: Herald Press, 2009). Permission is granted to reprint this prayer for a single congregational use.

A prayer in response to 9/11

(can be used in context of violence and loss of life)

God of all comfort, we confess our bewilderment,
our sadness, anger, and fear.
Hear our prayers.
Surround those who mourn the loss of loved ones.
Embrace them with your loving arms.
Comfort those who long for the missing.
Carry them in your loving arms.

Protect those who risk their lives in rescue efforts.
Strengthen them with your loving arms.
Remind us that your love is stronger than hate.
Keep us from becoming the evil we deplore.
Give us wisdom and restraint.
With trembling faith we pray, O God,
    for a sure sense of your presence in our grieving.
Embrace us with your loving arms.
In you alone do we trust. Amen.

By Carmen Schrock-Hurst. From *Words for Worship 2* (Scottdale, PA and Waterloo, ON: Herald Press, 2009). Permission is granted to reprint this prayer for a single congregational use.

Prayer after a disaster

Merciful God, the pain of this day is beyond comprehension.
People's homes are lost and family members are dead
    because of this terrible disaster.
In our sorrow, in our fear, yes, even in our anger,
    we look to you for comfort and solace,
    the Creator of heaven and earth.
Comfort, O comfort your people!
Join our cries to the groans of creation
    that all will be made whole in you.
  (*prayer for people who have lost property or loved ones*)

In this dark time, we remember that you walk with us
    and wrap your comforting arms around us.
Go with us as we begin the work of picking up the pieces.
Grant us the strength found in your community.
We pray in the name of our Lord and Savior, Jesus Christ. Amen.

By Joel Short. From *Words for Worship 2* (Scottdale, PA and Waterloo, ON: Herald Press, 2009). Permission is granted to reprint this prayer for a single congregational use.

Prayer for a time of crisis

(based on Psalm 121; 27; Psalm 46:1-3, Matthew 6:26-30; 10:29–31)

O Lord, you are our light and our salvation.
Who, or what, shall we fear?
Our help comes from you, O Lord.
We lift our gaze to your mountains,
to the birds of the air and the flowers of the field.
We know that you number the very hairs of our head.
Therefore, we will not fear.
We know we are of more value than the birds and the flowers,
and if you care for them, you will surely care for us.
You are our keeper, our defense.
We will wait on you.
We will be strong and let our hearts take courage.
We will not be anxious for tomorrow, nor will we fear,
though the earth should change, or the mountains quake,
or the waters roar and foam.
For you know what we need.
You are our refuge and strength,
our present help in trouble. Amen.

By Esther Lanting. From Indiana-Michigan Anthology. 2000 of the Indiana-Michigan Mennonite Conference. Permission is granted for congregational use of this prayer.

Prayer after a tragedy

After a tragedy, words are inadequate. Worshippers should be oriented to the silence and meditation that is at the heart of this prayer, based on Psalm 56.

You have kept count of our tossings, O Lord,
you have put our tears in your bottle.
Are they not in your record?
(Moments of silence. Then invite worshippers to imagine God kneeling beside their beds at night, catching their tears and making notes about their suffering.)

Today when we call, this we know:
that God is for us.
(Moments of silence. Then invite worshippers to consider how God has been present for them in the past despite their current loss and pain.)

In God, whose word we praise,
in the Lord, whose name we honor,
in God we trust; we are not afraid. Amen.
(Free spoken prayers. Then invite worshippers to reaffirm confidence and trust in God.)

By Elaine Maust. Meridian, Mississippi. From *Words for Worship 2* (Scottdale, PA and Waterloo, ON: Herald Press, 2009). Permission is granted to reprint this prayer for a single congregational use.

Grounded in God's love

Lord, as we gather today, in our ordinary way in your presence, and in the presence of one another, we are all too aware that much is amiss in the world. We are all too aware, that even in this quiet moment, some of your beloved people and parts of your beloved earth are being visited by death and destruction.

For the sake of the world you love, we pray that our simple commitment to the routines of worship will not be an escape from life but a sacrament of hope that turns us back to the needs of the world, more grounded in your love.

May our attention to ordinary things be a way of saying that we trust you as the one who cradles the world and its people in your all-embracing arms. In Jesus' name, Amen.

Mary H. Schertz, Elkhart, Indiana. Permission is granted to reprint this prayer for a single congregational use.

Worship Services

The following plans are for three worship services that would occur: 1) in anticipation of a pandemic or other health crisis; 2) in the midst of such a crisis; and 3) in the aftermath of the crisis. The services can also be adapted for use during other crises, such as natural disasters or outbreaks of violence.

Additional worship resources can be gleaned from the stories and Scripture reflections of the study book, *Beyond our Fears: Following Jesus in Times of Crisis*, and from the accompanying adult and youth leader guides included in this volume (pages 11 and 39).

Worship Service

In Anticipation of a Potential Health Crisis

Focus: Preparation for a crisis is both a sign of wisdom and an act of service.

Scripture texts: Genesis 6:14-16, 18-22; Romans 12:9-13

Visual elements: On the worship table place an illustration of Noah's ark or items used for emergencies (*first aid kit, jugs of water, etc.*) as illustrations of "preparedness."

Gathering

Call to worship

L: We want to serve the Lord.
P: But we are distracted by many things.
L: There is much to be done
P: and now is the time to prepare.
L: O God, grant us wisdom to serve you
P: and to do your will. Amen.

Hymn: "Come, let us all unite to sing" (Text attributed to Howard Kingsbury)

Opening prayer

All-wise God, we gather to worship you today. We come to listen for your wisdom, to examine our hearts, discern our actions, and to celebrate your ongoing love for us. Move among us, gracious and wise God. Amen.

Praising

Hymns with an emphasis on wisdom and service.

Prayer of thanksgiving

We give you thanks, O God, for your faithful love endures forever. It is in you that we live and breathe and have our being. You are life itself. We praise your holy name, Amen.

Confessing

Hymn: "Brothers and sisters of mine" (text by Kenneth I. Morse)

Prayer of confession

Loving God, it is easy for us to choose to ignore the signs and warnings of approaching danger. We fear uncertainty and we lack trust. We lose our focus to do what you want us to do. We are unprepared, thinking we have plenty of time to do what needs to be done. Honestly, we are overwhelmed by the needs and demands of today and are reluctant to look forward to the challenges of tomorrow. We forget to trust you with our daily concerns.

Forgive us our own shortsightedness, our own foolishness. Grant us your wisdom and vision, and help us to act on your behalf. In Jesus' name we pray. Amen.

Words of assurance:

God's promises are true! God loves us and is faithful to forgive us. God promises to pour out wisdom and faithfulness to us. God's promises are true and can be trusted! Live boldly, trusting God's word.

Hearing

Children's time

Supplies: stuffed animals to load up onto the ark; a rain stick to create the sound of rain.

Dramatize the story of Noah with all the children and a few adult volunteers. Invite the children to pretend to be Noah's family building the ark (use chairs for construction) and moving the stuffed animals onto the ark. While this is happening the adult volunteers poke gentle fun at Noah, either from their seats, or from up front. The adults wonder why Noah is doing such a seemingly crazy thing as to build an ark in a dry field without any storm clouds visible in the sky.

Focus on Noah's willingness to do what God asked him to do even if it seemed silly and people made fun of him. Remind the children that despite the teasing from Noah's neighbors, Noah kept doing what God commanded.

Scripture reading: Genesis 6:14-16, 18-22; Romans 12:9-13

Sermon starters

The story of Noah offers an example of preparation as both a sign of wisdom and an act of service. Noah prepares the ark out of obedience to God, a sign of wisdom. This obedience took Noah's time, involved his family, and made Noah appear delusional. He continued to build the ark despite the evidence that floods did not occur in his area. His faithfulness ultimately revealed his wisdom.

The Romans passage encourages us to serve others in wisdom. We are to serve others out of trust in God rather than out of fear of a disaster. When we do not prepare, we ignore or limit our opportunities to serve our neighbors.

Are we willing to prepare for a possible pandemic and risk looking foolish to others? Are we able to prepare as an act of trust rather than fear? How might we anticipate the needs of the community as an act of love for both God and the community?

Hymn of response: "Forth in thy name" (text by Charles Wesley)

Prayers of the congregation

Holy God, we bring before you our concerns, fears, and confusion. We lay them before you and ask you to respond to our requests. We pray for courage to prepare in the face of misunderstanding by others; help us to be brave. We pray for wisdom and prudence in the way we prepare for crisis; give us common sense, focus, and understanding among ourselves. We pray that our hearts will be willing to be faithful to your call to prepare; give eyes to see and ears to hear your will and direction. Finally, Holy God, we pray for those persons and communities who are at risk today; through your people, give them many signs of you love and hope. We pray all of these things in Jesus' holy name, your son and our savior, Amen.

Hymn: "Master, let me walk with thee" (text by Washington Gladden) or "Spirit of the living God" (text and music: Daniel Iverson)

Sending

Benediction:

Get ready! Go into God's world with wisdom and boldness to do God's will. Go in peace knowing God's peace will be with you. Amen.

Worship Service

During a Health Crises

Focus: God reminds us to "fear not," trusting that God is with us.

Scripture texts: Deuteronomy 31:6-13; Psalm 4:8; Isaiah 41:10; Luke 2:10; for children's time: 1 Samuel 17

Visual elements: Place a light blue cloth over the worship table. Light as many candles as needed to represent persons or families in the congregation impacted by the health crisis.

Gathering

Call to worship

L: Fear not!
P: God is with us.
L: Fear not!
P: We trust in God.
L: Fear not!
P: We trust God is with us.
L: Alleluia!
ALL: Alleluia! Amen!

Hymn: "There is a place of quiet rest" (text by Cleland B. McAfee)

Opening prayer

Loving God, we thank you for the privilege of worshipping together, even during a time of worry and uncertainty. During this time we ask that you meet us in our fears. Impress upon us that you are with us always and we don't need to be afraid. We ask for hearts open to you this day. In Jesus' name we pray. Amen.

Praising

Hymns that emphasize trust in God

Confessing

Hymn: "Out of the depths I cry to you" (text by Martin Luther, based on Psalm 130)

Prayer of confession

Gracious and loving God, even though you tell us not to be afraid, we are afraid. We are fearful to go beyond our familiar places. We want to control our environment. We are anxious when we are around strangers. Forgive us. Forgive our fears. Forgive our lack of trust in your providential care. Forgive our retreat into ourselves, and our insensitivity to those who around us who are suffering, who worry, who struggle to have faith. Have mercy on us, O God.

(silence)

Words of assurance

Hear the good news: Fear not! We are reconciled to God, who is worthy of our trust. Rejoice! God's love is poured out to you, now and forever, through Jesus Christ, Amen.

Hearing

Children's time

Supplies needed: Children's Bible, hand sanitizer, facial tissues

Summarize the story of David from 1 Samuel 17 when he faces a lion and Goliath. Emphasize how God prepared him to do scary things, like face a lion and giant. Remind them God's with them and watching over them, but God is also preparing them if they have to face this illness. God prepares us when we do things to protect ourselves and others from sickness: through washing hands thoroughly, covering mouths when coughing, using tissues. (Demonstrate these measures as you describe them). Because David was prepared he was able to trust God and be brave.

Scripture reading: Deuteronomy 31:6-13; Isaiah 41:10; Luke 2:10

Sermon starters

In the Isaiah text, there are expressions of God's continual presence with God's people. The recurring promise of God's presence is the most fundamental assurance given to us: God is with us. These announcements radically transform situations by causing us to be aware of God's constant presence and therefore less fearful.

Hymn of response: "How firm a foundation" (text by John Rippon)

Prayers of the congregation

The congregational response can include a short song such as "Healer of our every ill" by Marty Haugen, or a unison response such as "O Lord, hear our prayer."

God who holds together all people and all situations in our world, we come to you with our concerns, worries, and fears. We offer them to you, knowing you listen to us as we pray together.

O God, we bring before you those who are sick [*name individuals*].
(congregational response)

O God, we pray for the families of those who are sick [*name family members known to the congregation*].
(congregational response)

O God, we bring before you all the medical personnel working to treat people [*name professionals known to the congregation and the community*].
(congregational response)

O God, we pray for our government leaders as they respond to this crisis [*name individuals in government with health oversight*].
(congregational response)

O God, we pray for our worshipping community. Help us to know how to respond with wisdom.
(congregational response)

O God, we thank you for listening and responding to our prayers. Amen.

Hymn: "O Love that will not let me go" (text by George Matheson) or "Prayer is the soul's sincere desire" (text by James Montgomery)

Sending

Benediction

Emmanuel, God with us,
As we leave this time of worship,
May we go, knowing that you will never leave us or forsake us.
Remind us throughout this next week that we can trust you with all that we are and all whom we hold dear. Amen.

Worship Service

In the Aftermath of a Health Crisis

Focus: God is with each of us in times of great tragedy.

Scripture texts: Psalm 28; Psalm 46:1-3; 2 Corinthians 1:3-7

Visual elements: A dark cloth covering the worship table with several lit candles.

Gathering

Call to worship (based on Palm 28)

L: To you, O Lord, we call,
do not turn a deaf ear to us.

P: **Hear our cry for mercy**
as we call to you for help,
as we lift up our hands
to you in your sanctuary.

L: The Lord is our strength and our shield;
in God our hearts trust.

P: **The Lord is our strength**
and our saving refuge.

All: O God, be our shepherd and carry us forever. Amen.

Hymn: "O God, our help in ages past" (text by Isaac Watts)

Opening prayer

O God, our Comforter, shock and sorrow is dominating our hearts and minds. Help us as we ponder the loss and the pain we have witnessed. We come to you in worship seeking your comfort and hope. We know you are present with us in this place. In Jesus' name, Amen.

Praising

Hymns that provide solace and comfort in times of deep pain. It may be appropriate to give opportunity for worshippers to suggest songs that are meaningful to them. Periods of silence might also be welcome at this time. Alternatively, choose music your congregation is comfortable singing with an emphasis on God's faithfulness and presence.

Confessing

Hymn: "From the depths of sin" (text by Willard F. Jabusch, based on Psalm 130)

(silence)

Prayer of confession

God of mercy, we need your grace and compassion. Our hearts are in turmoil. Forgive us where we have sinned—either intentionally or unintentionally, through our actions or by ignoring those in need. We ask for your Spirit to work in us so that we might bring your healing and hope to comfort everyone in need. In Jesus' name we pray, Amen.

Words of assurance

Our God is a merciful God, who loves us and is faithful to forgive us. Trust God to offer you healing and hope at this time of loss and disappointment. God is with you. Amen.

(silence)

Hearing

Children's time

Supplies: Newsprint and drawing/writing tools.

Invite the children to sit in a circle so all can hear and see each other. Then talk with them (not to them) about their impressions and understandings of the tragedy. Ask them: Does anyone know what happened this week? Did you talk about it at home/school? What do you think about what happened?

Offer the children the paper and drawing tools to take with them back to their seats. Invite the children to draw pictures of what they most remember during the past few days or weeks.

Pray for the children and the concerns they mentioned. Invite them to say short prayers as well. Remind them that Jesus is with them and that they can talk to Jesus any time about the tragedy.

Sermon starters

This is a time to remind the congregation that God is with them in the midst of their pain, shock, and sorrow. One suggestion is to weave the biblical stories of God's presence with the Israelites together with congregational stories of God's presence with persons who experienced a crisis (with permission). Reflect on God's continual presence even "though the earth should change," (Psalm 46:2). Underscore God's promises to "console us in our afflictions" (2 Corinthians 1:4). The sermon might be short, given the other elements of the worship service.

Prayers of the congregation

Adapt the prayer to the specific situation you are in. The congregational response can be silence, spoken individual prayers, a unison prayer of "Lord, hear our prayer," or a sung response of "O Lord, hear my prayer" (Taize song based on Psalm 102:1-2) or "Lord, listen to your children" (text by Ken Medema).

Emmanuel, God who is with us, with confidence we offer our prayers to you on behalf of a world turned upside down. We especially pray for the people most directly impacted by this crisis. Gather them under your wings, calm their fears, and keep their faith strong.
(congregational response)

We pray for those who are grieving the loss of family members, friends, and communities, for those separated and searching for family members, for those who are in shock. We ask for your continual healing presence to each of them.
(congregational response)

We offer to you all those who are involved with recovery efforts—for the medical staff and counselors working with the sick, the injured, the traumatized. Be with caregivers in local churches as they minister to their communities. Give them strength and stamina during this time of stress.
(congregational response)

We pray for those who are preparing to rebuild the community's functions—for government personnel and service organizations who must work together with efficiency and fair-mindedness. We pray for clarity of mind, listening hearts, and clear communication.
(congregational response)

Finally, Emmanuel God, we pray for our neighbors and friends as they support one another to rebuild their community and truly be a community once again. Bring them peace and protection from all evil. We ask all these things in the name of God our Creator, Jesus our Redeemer, and the Holy Spirit our Sustainer. Amen.

Hymn: "My life flows on" (text by Robert Lowry)

Sending

Hymn: "Amazing Grace!" (text by John Newton)

Benediction

Go now from this place knowing God has heard our grief. Continue to pray for families who have lost loved ones, and for those who grieve, and for those in positions to help. Together let us find ways to act in love toward all. Amen.

Initial Steps Congregations Can Take to Prepare for a Pandemic*

A. The congregation's leadership body should conduct an **initial review** of their theological basis for responding to a pandemic, and then determine if the congregation should embrace a preparedness plan.

B. If yes, then the leadership body should appoint a **pandemic preparedness working group** from within the congregation. The group should be composed of a pastor, spiritual caregiver; a worship committee member; a healthcare professional if available; a custodian or facilities trustee; a finance person; and a communications officer.

C. The pandemic preparedness working group should develop a **congregational plan** that flows out of the following tasks:

1. Review in some detail the resources and literature on the impacts of health emergencies such as a pandemic. For local resources they should contact municipal and health institutions. Other resources are listed on pages 102-3 of this guide and at www.churchpandemicresources.ca.
2. Contact regional health officials to understand existing public health plans, approaches, and resource people.
3. Collaborate with these groups to share information and plans, establish communication links, and explore opportunities outside the congregation to be of service and extend the critical mass.
4. Hold a series of initial **congregational conversations** (see below) to explore and answer important questions about potential congregation-wide engagement in this initiative.
5. Develop a plan for the congregation to prepare for a local health emergency based on the impact such an emergency could have on various congregational functions, especially:
   - caring ministries and mutual aid
   - business function of the congregation, including staffing issues
   - worship and education.

* Adapted from the Mennonite Church Canada pandemic preparedness website: www.churchpandemicresources.ca

6. Engage public health agencies, other neighborhood churches, and community resources to help with practical organization and education.
7. In collaboration with the education committee, worship committee and care group leaders, develop a plan for congregational education (adults, youth, and children) and for specialized practical training in pandemic response.

D. The working group will present the plans to the congregation's leadership body for discussion, congregational approval, and implementation.

Some questions for congregational conversations

Vision and mission

- In what ways could a major health emergency impact our congregation?
- What does it mean as a follower of Christ to help others in need during a crisis, even if it means placing oneself in harm's way to do so?

Information

- Is the church contact list current?
- Who are the healthcare professionals and spiritual caregivers within our congregation?
- Who in our congregation relates to other neighborhood churches/faith groups?
- Which local health authorities should we contact regarding community emergency plans?
- What other community groups, ministerial committees, and interfaith councils, do we need to be in touch with?
- Who are the people in our congregation who will be most vulnerable to a crisis? Do we know where they live?
- Who outside our congregation depends on us for services, programs, and other resources or support? How will we stay supportive?
- Who lives in the immediate neighborhood of the church meeting place, and who among them are the most vulnerable during an emergency?
- Who in the congregation will be available to fill in for our pastors and church staff in the event some fall ill in a pandemic?

Strategy

- How will we mobilize existing groups in our congregation instead of creating new caring structures?
- When a pandemic puts extra pressure on pastors, church staff, and leaders, how will we care for them and their families?
- Will we close our doors until a pandemic is over?
- Which ministries will we need to suspend during a pandemic? Will we continue to do only spiritual ministry and curtail other church and community programs? Will we do only humanitarian activities?
- Will we reach out broadly, or will we minister only to our own people?
- Will we work by ourselves, with sister churches, or with the community?
- What methods are available to communicate within the congregation and with neighbors, reliably, accurately, and in a timely way, when normal communication is curtailed?

Hymns cited in this guide

For those who use *Hymnal: A Worship Book*, the hymnal of Mennonite Publishing Network, and its supplements, the following list gives the hymn numbers.

HWB = *Hymnal: A Worship Book*
STJ = *Sing the Journey* (HWB supplement 1)
STS = *Sing the Story* (HWB supplement 2)

Amazing Grace (HWB 143)
Brothers and sisters of mine (HWB 142)
Calm me, Lord (STS 45)
Come, bring your burdens to God (STS 50)
Come, let us all unite to sing (HWB 12)
Come, walk with us (STJ 2)
From the depths of sin (HWB 136)
Healer of our every ill (HWB 377)
Help us to help each other (HWB 362)
Here I am, Lord (HWB 395)
How firm a foundation (HWB 567)
I am weak and I need thy strength by (HWB, 553)
In the bulb there is a flower (HWB 614)
In your sickness, your sufferings (HWB 585)
Keep me safe, O God (STJ 50)
Make me a channel of your peace (STJ 56)
My life flows on (HWB 580)
O God, our help in ages past (HWB 328)
O master, let me walk with thee (HWB 357)
Out of the depths I cry to you (HWB 133)
There is a place of quiet rest (HWB 5)
Spirit of the living God (HWB 349)
This little light of mine (HWB 401)
When peace, like a river (HWB, 336)
When the poor ones (STJ 69)
When the storms of life are raging (HWB 558)
Will you come and follow me? (STS 39)
Will you let me be your servant (HWB 307)

Resources

Books

Long, Laurie Ecklund. *My Life in a Box: A Life Organizer*. Fresno, CA: AGL Publishing, 2008. Practical ways families can organize their important papers and possessions so they are ready when a major crisis comes.

Light Our Way: A Guide for Spiritual Care in Times of Disaster. NVOAD (National Volunteer Organizations Active in Disasters) 2006. This 66-page guide is available for download at: www.nvoad.org/Portals/0/Light_Our_Way_LINKS.pdf

New Every Day: Forty Devotions for Disaster Survivors. Evangelical Lutheran Church in America, 2007. For a free copy, phone Augsburg Fortress at (800) 328-4648.

Meeting God in the Ruins: Devotions for Disaster Relief Volunteers. Evangelical Lutheran Church in America, 2003. For a free copy, phone Augsburg Fortress at (800) 328-4648.

O'Keefe, Betty and Ian Macdonald. *Dr. Fred and the Spanish Lady: Fighting the Killer Flu.* Surrey, BC: Heritage House, 2004. Tells of Dr. Fred Underhill and his battle against the 1918 Spanish influenza that killed 25 to 50 million people worldwide—a compelling story of people coming together in a crisis.

Ramirez, Frank. *Here I Am: Brethren Disaster Ministries Devotional Guide*. Church of the Brethren General Board, 2007. Available online at: www.brethren.org Follow the links behind "Serve."

Roberts, Stephen B. and Willard W. C. Ashley, eds. *Disaster Spiritual Care: Practical Clergy Responses to Community*, Regional and National Tragedy. Woodstock, VT: Skylight Paths Publishing, 2008. The definitive guidebook for counseling not only the victims of disaster but also the spiritual leaders who are called to service in the wake of a crisis.

Stark, Rodney. *The Rise of Christianity: A Sociologist Reconsiders History*. Princeton: Princeton University Press, 1996. Includes fascinating history of the witness and growth of the second- and third-century church during the international plagues that occurred throughout the Roman Empire.

CD

Faith Community Summit on Pandemic Preparedness and Response (Mennonite Church Canada; available through its resource center, below). Coverage of the first-ever national forum of its kind in Canada, in 2007. Includes addresses by healthcare experts, government officials, and faith community leaders about the role faith groups will play during a major health emergency.

Websites

Church Pandemic Resources
Most often referenced in *Beyond our Fears Guide for Leaders*
www.churchpandemicresources.ca
A Mennonite online resource to help congregations prepare for and respond in the event of a pandemic. Sponsored by Mennonite Church Canada and Mennonite Disaster Service, the site has many resources and additional links.

Mennonite Disaster Service
www.mds.mennonite.net
The volunteer Anabaptist organization that offers a helping hand and a Christian witness in the wake of domestic natural disasters and other crises. Search specifically at http://mds.mennonite.net/fileadmin/Resources/Preparing_for_Disaster_Mar_07_Full_page.pdf for *Preparing for Disaster: A Guide for Mennonite Congregations.*

Mennonite Church Canada Resource Centre
www.mennonitechurch.ca/resourcecentre/Home
Search by "disaster" or "pandemic" to find books and videos listed here. Resources are available to Canadians for loan.

Eden Extension Disaster Network
www.eden.lsu.edu/LearningOps/FBO
This link is for faith-based organizations dealing with pandemics and other disasters. The website has many other links to help communities and governments prepare for crisis.

Evangelical Lutheran Church of America Disaster Response
http://www.elca.org/disaster
For pandemic resources, follow links to "Faithful Preparation for Pandemic Flu."

Acknowledgments

Overall direction for this Leader's Guide and its associated books, *Beyond our Fears* and *Don't Be Afraid*, came from a steering group comprised of Gord Friesen, facilitator of the Mennonite Church Canada Pandemic Preparedness Task Force; Lois Nickel, Director of Region Relations and Programs for Mennonite Disaster Service; Janet Plenert, Executive Secretary of Mennonite Church Canada Witness; and series editor Byron Rempel-Burkholder of Faith & Life Resources. Special thanks go to a network of consultants who gave us ideas and story leads—especially Alan Kreider, Carol Ringer, and Nomusa Chikari. Funding for the series was generously provided by Mennonite Disaster Service.

Adult and Youth Study Guides

Pam Driedger, the author of the participant book, *Beyond our Fears: Following Jesus in Times of Crisis*, provided the Scriptural framework and many of the ideas for the sessions. Carol Duerksen and Eleanor Snyder added to the material and put the guides into the final format for the youth and adult guides respectively. Driedger is Director of Spiritual Care at Manitoba's Eden Mental Health Centre, and speaks and writes on the church's role in health and healing. Duerksen, formerly editor of *With*, currently is writing junior youth Sunday school curriculum for Gather 'Round. Snyder is director of Faith & Life Resources.

Children's Activities

Rebecca Seiling and Cindy Snider provided most of the material, based on the stories they wrote in *Don't Be Afraid: Stories of Christians in Times of Trouble*. Eleanor Snyder and Byron Rempel-Burkholder provided additional material, and put it all into a consistent form. Seiling and Snider have written a variety of children's materials—most recently *Plant a Seed for Peace*, and *Finding Anna Bee* respectively.

Congregational Prayers for Times of Crisis

These came from a variety of sources, and most are also included in the Herald Press worship book: *Words for Worship 2*, edited by Diane Zaerr Brenneman. Credits are given beneath each piece.

Worship Services

June Mears Driedger, editor of *Leader* magazine, wrote the three services.